INSIGHT C

CYPRUS

Compact Guide: Cyprus is the ultimate quick-reference guide to this popular destination. It tells you all you need to know about the island's attractions, from ancient legends to modern passions, idyllic sandy beaches to rugged peninsulas, dense forests to defiant castles and remote mountain monasteries to bustling cities.

This is one of 133 Compact Guides, combining the interests and enthusiasms of two of the world's best-known information providers: Insight Guides, whose innovative titles have set the standard for visual travel guides since 1970, and Discovery Channel, the world's premier source of nonfiction television programming.

Discovery Channel

APA PUBLICATIONS
Part of the Langenscheidt Publishing Group

Star Attractions

An instant reference to some of Cyprus's most popular tourist attractions to help you on your way.

Nicosia p16

Kourion p42

Rock of Aphrodite p44

Pafos p46

Agios Neofytos p52

Mt Olympos p57

Keryneia (Girne) p59

Morfou (Güzelyurt) p61

Panagia tou Araka p30

Buffavento Castle p67

Salamis p72

Introduction

Places

Culture

Leisure

Practical Information

Cyprus – Aphrodite's Island

According to Homer, the goddess Aphrodite, 'born of the sea foam', came ashore on Cyprus. The goddess of love and beauty knew that she had chosen a beautiful island surrounded by turquoise sea and washed by gentle waves, where the sun shines almost all year round, and with a backdrop of spectacular rocks and tall mountains offering shady, cool woodland for her to enjoy the company of the gods.

We know little of Aphrodite's encounters with mere mortals, but she would certainly have received a warm welcome. Cypriot hospitality is characterised by the Greek word *kopiaste*, which roughly translated means: 'Come in, sit down and join us'. There is always a good reason to celebrate – a marriage, perhaps, or a baptism. A Sunday afternoon picnic is another popular occasion for families to enjoy a generous combination of food, drink, dance and song, and guests will quickly be made to feel at home.

Cyprus offers more than sunbathing and cultural heritage. While holidaymakers are browning on the beach during the first hot days of spring, Cypriots up in the Troodos mountains may be out on the slopes with their skis. In the Mesaoria (Mesarya), cistus, anemones and wild leek bloom as early as December, and when the mountain region is at its coldest, the plain is smothered in pink almond blossom.

In the South, the Akamas peninsula with its exotic flora and the Troodos, with their fruit groves, woods and crystal-clear mountain streams, make ideal walking country. In the North, nature-lovers should not miss a tour of the Pentadaktylos (Beşparmak) mountains and the Karpasia (Kirpaşa) peninsula. Only man disturbs the peaceful natural environment. The Cypriots' current favourite toy is the four-wheel-drive, used to reach remote picnic sites. Bulldozers have brutally transformed bridle paths into wide tracks suitable for these powerful vehicles. While the North is still largely unspoilt as a result of poverty and political isolation, the South has suffered from the demands of the motorist and the property developer.

One hotel manager believes that, if the holidaymakers are to keep coming, Cyprus 'must retain its uniqueness, its natural environment, its villages, its customs and its traditions'. In much of the South all of these attributes have been degraded by the recent boom decades.

Location and landscape

The Cypriots regard themselves as Europeans, but geographically the island of Cyprus, situated between Turkey and Egypt, belongs to Asia Minor. With the Karpasia peninsula pointing to the northeast, ancient historians described the outline of the island as an opened-out sheep-

Opposite: Buffavento Castle

Picnic time

Konnos Bay

Ripe for the picking

skin. About 20 million years ago, during the Miocene era, the pressure of the continental plates raised the Troodos mountains to the surface of what is now the Mediterranean. Wind and rain carried away the soft sedimentary rock, exposing the massif which consists of hard, compacted effusive rock from deep inside the earth's crust. For geologists, the Troodos and Mount Olympos (1,951m/ 6,400ft), Cyprus's highest peak, serve as a classic illustration of the earth's history.

The second range, the long and narrow Pentadaktylos or Five Finger mountains (1,023m/ 3,355ft) emerged from the sea to the north of the island. The two ranges were initially just isolated islands rearing out of shallow water, but sediment such as chalk, marl and sandstone accumulated and formed the present-day Mesaoria plain. Gradually, the water level sank, and about three million years ago the two mountain ranges became linked, creating the island of Cyprus as it is today. The finishing touch, as it were, was added by the formation of a coastal reef made up of dead coral, millions of years old.

Akamas coastline and the Pentadaktylos mountains

The total area of the island is 9,251sq km (3,570sq miles) with 3,450sq km (1,331sq miles) under Turkish administration. 'Sovereign British Bases' occupy 257sq km (100sq miles). The capital of Cyprus is Nicosia (Lefkosia/ Lefkoşa), Greek pop. 210,000; Turkish pop. 50,000. Other major towns include Limassol (Lemesos), pop. 165,000; Larnaka, pop. 75,000; Pafos, pop. 50,000; and Famagusta (Ammochostos/Gazimağusa), pop. 30,000.

Hot weather for goat herding

Climate and when to go

The Mediterranean climate bestows on Cyprus mild, damp winters and warm, dry summers in which the bright sun and clear light give colours a startling intensity. Only the Troodos mountains enjoy a pleasantly cool climate in the summer, and there are modest opportunities for skiing here when snow falls between December and February.

In the spring the otherwise arid and parched land shows its green and fertile side, although in April the weather can be changeable and the sea is still cold. The ideal month for a visit has to be May. By June the new growth is beginning to turn that characteristic brownish yellow. However, with temperature differences between day and night averaging 15°C/59°F, a jumper and rainwear are needed to supplement light, cotton summer clothing.

In the summer Cypriots and walkers appreciate the cool mountain air. At lower altitudes the heat is conducive only to lazy hours by the pool or on the beach, although the shade of a parasol and the fresh wind that often blows in the late morning render the heat by the coast bearable, and the balmy evenings are a delight. The summer climate on the Mesaoria plain, however, can be unpleasantly hot. Light, summer clothing is fine for the beach at all times of day but, even in July, take a sweatshirt on a trip into the mountains. The dry summer lasts into October, sometimes even November, but then suddenly, without an autumn interlude, the rainy season starts. Many hotels and restaurants close. Of the hotels that remain open, only the better establishments have heating, while in the bars customers tend to gather around the stove. Although Cypriot winters are mild by northern European standards, warm clothing is advisable, given the damp air. For winter breaks, the best areas are in the west and along the southern coastline.

Nature and environment

With such a variety of landscape and the regional differences in climate, Cyprus is a paradise for amateur botanists. There are still areas not fully explored, and nature-lovers will make some surprising discoveries. Species unique to the island are plentiful with 110 recorded so far, including the Cyprus cotton thistle and rare orchids such as the Cyprus bee orchid *(ophrys kotschyi)*. The carob, a common species on Cyprus, is rarely found elsewhere; its close relatives died out during the Ice Age.

Prickly pear

In low-lying areas, the tall, chest-high maquis or *phrygana* is a common feature of the Cypriot landscape. Weeds, shrubs and bushes create a colourful community of plants. Against a background landscape that may well be grey and monotone, the yellow broom stands out brightly. Many herbs, such as bay, rosemary, sage, thyme, mint and marjoram, can be detected from their aroma, and the Cypriots have come to appreciate these plants for their medicinal as well as culinary properties. Walkers on the Akamas and Karpasia peninsulas will be able to study the plant life in the *phrygana* more closely.

Goat with an appetite and Aleppo Pine

Desecration of natural features is nothing new in the modern world, but the practice can be traced back to antiquity. By the Middle Ages ore extraction and shipbuilding had reduced the woods of Cyprus to a wasteland. Voracious mountain goats nibbling away at the young saplings have also played their part, and now the woods are unable to renew themselves independently. Nevertheless, Cyprus can claim to be one of the most densely wooded islands in the Mediterranean. In the last century, large-scale re-afforestation was seen as a solution to soil erosion. The forestry experts have often chosen the quick-growing and undemanding Aleppo pine *(pinus brutia),* which appreciates the acid soil. This tree now constitutes about 90 percent of the island's tree stocks. Only in one or two remote spots, such as in the 'Valley of the

Fishing out of Agia Napa

Facing the world head on

Cedars' have the endemic Troodos cedars *(cedrus libani ssp. brevifolia)* survived. The once-threatened moufflon *(ovis ammon orientalis)* have their homes in these woods, although visitors are unlikely to experience a close encounter with these shy mountain sheep in the wild. They can, however, be seen in Limassol's zoo and at the Stavros tis Psokas forest station in the Pafos forest. The moufflon appears on the island's coat-of-arms.

Increasing pollution in the Mediterranean and the development of sandy beaches for tourism has seriously restricted the natural habitat of the marine loggerhead turtle, *caretta caretta*, and the green turtle, *chelonia mydas*. Although the animals are protected species and there are projects in both North and South to protect a few breeding beaches, only one out of every 4,000 young turtles that are born will reach maturity and produce their own young. Signs are posted on the beaches asking the public to take due care.

Population and religion

By looking at old maps of the island's colonial past in which the original Turkish and Greek settlements are shown in different colours, it becomes clear how widely the two groups had integrated. In many towns and villages both communities lived alongside each other in harmony. After the troubles of 1963/64 the Turks withdrew into enclaves and sealed-off quarters in the towns, but following the Turkish invasion *(see page 13)* both Greeks and Turks were forced to move out into separate areas. Cyprus had undergone its own process of 'ethnic cleansing'.

Today there are only two villages in the Greek sector which have a mixed population: Potamia and Pyla, although small Turkish Cypriot communities live in other parts of the South. In the North several hundred elderly Greeks continue to reside on the Karpasia peninsula.

Even if anyone knows how many people live on the island of Cyprus, the politicians on both sides of the divide keep the figures secret. The last 'all-island' census took place in 1960 and the statistics form an important element in discussions about the Cyprus problem, but the numbers have been extrapolated and probably over-estimated. Calculations originating in the South yield a figure of 735,000 Cypriots, 77 percent of whom are Orthodox, that is ethnic Greek, 18 percent are Muslim, i.e. Turkish, and the remainder are from the smaller religious communities such as Armenians, Maronites and Catholics.

The Turkish Cypriot northern part of the island has just over 160,000 inhabitants, not including the 35,000 Turkish soldiers stationed there. The main bone of contention is the fact that at least 60,000 Turks from the mainland have now settled on the island and the Greek Cypriots refuse to accept them as *bona fide* Turkish Cypriots. At the same time, somewhere in the region of 40,000 long-established Turkish Cypriots have left the island because of the depressed economic situation.

Cyprus has an ethnic problem, not a religious one. The religious ties of the native Cypriot Muslims are surprisingly weak. Anyone who takes a look inside Nicosia's Selimiye Mosque during Friday prayers will see that attendance is poor. On the streets, hardly any Turkish women wear the traditional headscarf. It is true that immigrants from the mainland are more deeply rooted in Islamic tradition. In their villages the otherwise rather casual observance of Ramadan, the month of fasting, is strictly enforced – it is impossible to buy even a cup of tea between sunrise and sunset.

Archbishop Makarios, president from 1960–77, was the last leader of the Greek Cypriots to combine the spiritual and political roles. The influence of the Greek Orthodox church on politics and the everyday life of the people has subsequently diminished. Unlike Roman Catholic priests, Greek Orthodox clerics are usually married. Bishops, however, are committed to celibacy, so elevation to the higher offices within the church is in practice restricted to monks. The reverence paid to icons *(see page 79)* and the pomp of the liturgy are perhaps the most striking features of the Orthodox church.

Customs

Religious traditions are still very much alive, even though Cypriots of the Orthodox community may not be as deeply religious these days as formerly. A great number of church festivals are celebrated, but their significance is rather different from what one might expect, for they feature a

Backgammon is Turkish

Growing up in Lefkara

Archbishop Makarios's tomb

Observing religious traditions

fascinating blend of pagan superstition and Christian rites.

Without doubt, the most important Orthodox Church festival is Easter, and no expense is spared in the celebrations. Preparations begin in earnest during Passion Week. On the eve of Easter Sunday, the whole village or local community arrives for Mass, equipped with an Easter egg and a candle. If there is no more room inside, latecomers assemble on the square in front of the church. When midnight strikes, the church door opens and the candles are lit. With the victory of Christ over death and evil, the festivities can begin. The cry '*Christos anesti!*' ('Christ is risen!') rings out, followed by the response '*Alethos anesti!*' ('Truly, He has risen!'). The Easter eggs, symbols of eternal life, are passed around and eaten, fireworks are lit, and then the congregation hurries away to continue the celebrations at home.

In the Muslim community, the circumcision ceremony welcoming the adolescent boy into the adult world is widely observed. Dressed in white, carrying a sceptre and wearing a crown, the youth is paraded through the streets like a prince, before the *sünnetçi* (circumciser) draws his knife and removes a part of the foreskin under local anaesthetic.

Economy

Over the past 40 years, southern Cyprus has metamorphosed from an underdeveloped, agricultural society into a modern finance and service centre, where the standard of living exceeds that of Greece. With continuing growth, full employment, a stable currency and negligible inflation, Cyprus is a model of economic success among the new wave of member states of the European Union that joined in 2004.

This economic miracle has, however, been evident mainly in the island's Greek Cypriot South. Even before 1974 *(see Historical Highlights, page 13)*, the Turks played only a minor role in the country's economic life. They were generally

Forging ahead in Limassol

less well educated and the larger concerns were owned by Greeks. Compared with Turkey, however, northern Cyprus is still relatively wealthy. Private individuals benefit from the remittances sent home by relatives in Britain and Australia. Many Cypriots continue to hope that both parties will appreciate the economic benefits that would accrue if the political barriers continue to be dismantled.

Gross domestic product in the Greek sector is more than four times that of the north. Tourism plays an important part in the island's economy with over 2 million visitors per year in the Greek Cypriot South, compared with about 100,000 in the North – but since the opening of the border in 2003, this latter figure of overseas arrivals has been supplemented by hundreds of thousands of visits by Greek Cypriots and people who are on holiday in the South.

City Plaza in Nicosia

Politics

Although the island has been split in two since 1974, in the eyes of the Greeks and according to international law the Republic of Cyprus is still undivided. Its parliament and government, made up only of Greek Cypriots, and the president, who is invested with wide-ranging powers, theoretically also represent Turkish Cypriots. The 'Turkish Republic of Northern Cyprus', or the 'pseudo-state' as it is scornfully described in the South, is officially recognised only by Turkey.

Since 1964 nearly 1,000 blue-helmeted United Nations soldiers have guarded the UN buffer zone in Nicosia, called the 'Green Line', between the Turkish and Greek zones. Their function is to supervise the cease-fire and to supply those Greek Cypriots and Maronites who remained in the North with food, medicines and other goods. Some 250sq km (100sq miles) of land around Akrotiri and Dekeleia on the southern coast of Cyprus still belongs to the UK under international law and the two British military bases there are of great strategic value.

Guarding the Green Line

The partial opening of the intra-island border in 2003, Cyprus joining the European Union in 2004 (only the South so far), and Turkey's progressing bid to join the EU have all injected new life and new dynamics into the search for a settlement. Not the least of the benefits of the border opening was the chance for Greek Cypriots and Turkish Cypriots (and Turkish migrants from the mainland) to meet each other in non-hostile situations. Yet also in 2004 the Greek Cypriots had voted against the UN's latest plan for reunification, and the Turkish Cypriots had voted in favour, reversing the usual situation where the Turkish Cypriots invariably took the international blame for failure. But the prospects for a settlement have clearly improved, and the EU is pressing hard for one. In 2005, the UN began new consultations about trying once more to achieve success.

Historical Highlights

9000–7000BC Stone tools and 'kitchen waste', excavated at Cape Gata, prove that Cyprus was inhabited during the Middle Stone Age by hunters and gatherers.

7000–3800BC In the Late Stone Age the first farms are established on the island.

3800–2500BC During the Copper Stone Age, the first tools, weapons and jewellery are produced from metal.

2500–1600BC Anatolian immigrants used to working with bronze settle on Cyprus. Towns such as Egkomi and Lapithos trade with Syria, Egypt and Asia Minor. Farmers use metal ploughshares, and the worship of bulls becomes widespread.

1600–1050BC Mycenaeans colonise Cyprus and Greek culture gains a foothold. The towns build huge Cyclopean walls to defend themselves against attacks from the 'Peoples of the Sea'.

1200BC onwards Extensive Aphrodite cult in Old Pafos.

1050–500BC During the Archaic period, ironworking gains appreciably in importance. The Phoenicians, based in Kition, establish a monopoly on external trade. Persians, Assyrians and Egyptians vie for political dominance. Royal tombs are built at Salamis.

700BC Assyrian king Sargon II subjugates the city kingdoms of Cyprus.

650BC Royal Tombs built at Tamassos.

540BC onwards Persian rule.

500–331BC Resistance against Persian rule preoccupies the islanders during much of the Classical period.

480BC At the Battle of Salamis, Cyprus joins the Persians against Athens.

411–374BC King Evagoras, who united the city-states from the city of Salamis, is unable to shake off the Persian yoke.

331–58BC At the beginning of the Hellenistic period, the Cypriot princes acclaim Alexander the Great as their liberator. Cyprus becomes a Hellenistic cultural province.

323BC Death of Alexander the Great. Cyprus becomes embroiled in various fights to succeed him.

312BC Zeno of Citium (Kition) founds Stoicism in Athens.

294BC The island falls under the control of the Egyptian Ptolemaic dynasty.

58BC Cyprus becomes a Roman province.

50BC onwards The beginning of the long period of peace, the *Pax Romana*.

AD45/46 The apostles Paul and Barnabas arrive as missionaries and convert the Roman governor Sergius Paulus to Christianity in Pafos. Temples to Apollo Hylates in Salamis, Soloi and Kourion are built.

115–117 Major Jewish uprising culminates in the expulsion of all Jews.

313 Christianity is recognised as an official religion of the Roman Empire.

332/342 Earthquake and famine devastate the island. Pafos and Salamis are destroyed, but Salamis is rebuilt and renamed 'Constantia'.

395 With the partition of the Roman Empire, Cyprus becomes part of the Byzantine Empire.

488 Emperor Zeno confirms the independence (*autokephalia*) of the Cypriot church.

649 Cyprus is occupied by the Arabs. By 688 it has to pay tribute to both the Byzantine Empire and the Caliphate.

730–843 The Iconoclastic Controversy rages over the use of religious images.

965–1185 Middle Byzantine Period. Cyprus flourishes. Churches and monasteries founded, and castles such as Buffavento.

1191 Richard the Lionheart conquers the island on his way to the Holy Land. He then sells it to the Knights Templar.

1192–1489 Cyprus passes to the French knight, Guy de Lusignan. Catholicism becomes the state religion.

1426 The island is overrun by raiders from Egypt, and forced to pay tribute to Cairo.

1489 Caterina Cornaro, widow of the last Lusignan king, James II, bequeaths Cyprus to the Venetian Republic.

1489–1571 Venetian rule. Byzantine painting flourishes around the turn of the century.

1571 Turkish troops under Mustafa Pasha occupy Cyprus, consequently part of the Ottoman Empire.

1660 The Sublime Porte bestows the right of independent representation upon bishops.

1774 The archbishop is recognised as the representative of the Christian population.

1821 Mainland Greece's war of liberation against Ottoman rule results in massacres, and looting against the Greeks in Cyprus.

1878 The Turks lease Cyprus to Great Britain.

1914 Britain annexes Cyprus.

1930s Economic boom. Attempts are made to unify Cyprus with Greece and to liberate the island from British rule.

1950 In a referendum organised by the Orthodox Church, 96 percent of Greek Cypriots vote for union with Greece (*enosis*).

1955 EOKA (National Organization of Cypriot Fighters) begins its campaign against British rule.

1960 The Republic of Cyprus is formed, with Archbishop Makarios as its first president.

1963 Makarios demands a constitutional amendment which the Turks perceive as a threat to their rights. First armed conflicts between the two ethnic groups, who begin to form enclaves.

1964 A United Nations peacekeeping force is stationed on Cyprus.

1974 Coup carried out against Makarios by the Cypriot National Guard. In July, Turkish troops invade the north of the island.

1983 Turkish Cypriots declare the north of the island the 'Turkish Republic of Northern Cyprus' but the new state is recognised only by Turkey.

1998 Negotiations on Cyprus joining the EU begin in Brussels.

1999 Cyprus is confirmed as a candidate for membership of the European Union, though without the support of the Turkish Cypriots.

2001 European Court of Human Rights finds Turkey guilty of widespread human rights violations arising from its 1974 invasion.

2003 The Green Line in Nicosia is opened to freer movement between the two sections.

2004 UN reunification plan put to referenda: Turkish Cypriots vote in favour and Greek Cypriots against. The Republic of Cyprus joins the European Union, but without the Turkish Cypriots.

2005 Cyprus joins Europe's revised Exchange Rate Mechanism, thereby paving the way for introduction of the euro, possibly by 2008.

Operation Attila

On 15 June 1974 the Athens military junta, supported by the Cyprus National Guard and a Greek regiment in Cyprus, initiated a coup against President Makarios. Apart from deflecting attention from Greece's domestic problems, one of the main objectives was to kill Makarios, but he escaped.

Nikos Sampson, the new leader, was held in contempt by the Turks, who remembered his exploits during the civil war when he was known as the 'Butcher of Omorphita'. A Turkish invasion force landed near Keryneia on 20 July 1974 and the Greek adventure ended in failure as the coup leaders surrendered. The Turkish operation, codenamed 'Attila', advanced as far as what is now the 'Green Line'. Over 6,000 Cypriots died during the coup and invasion, and a third of the population became refugees in their own country as a process of 'ethnic cleansing' began.

the king's house

HOTEL BRITISH
ERGENEKON

Preceding pages: Keryneia/Girne harbour

Life on the streets in Nicosia

Route 1

★★★ Nicosia (Lefkosia/Lefkoşa) – the divided capital

When the border between the two halves of Cyprus cut its way through the centre of Nicosia, what was once the heart of the old town found itself at the periphery. However, a city development plan devised by the European Union is attempting to smooth the path to re-unification. The smart pedestrian zones which follow a north–south axis – interrupted by the border – resemble each other both in colour and design, and the historically important but long-neglected residential quarters near the demarcation line display a new splendour. More importantly, since the opening of the Green Line at the UN's Ledra Palace Hotel crossing point in 2003 economic, social and personal links are being forged across the line in both directions. It is slowly becoming possible to begin to view Nicosia as a whole again, and the unnatural barrier of the demarcation line as an irritating anachronism rather than as the single most significant, and oppressive, element in the city's geography.

Despite its many monuments and historical buildings, Nicosia cannot compete with the seaside resorts. Even the locals take every opportunity to leave this inland city during the hot summer months. The best advice to those who wish to explore the city during the summer is to make a day trip.

History

During antiquity the small town of Ledra, as Nicosia was then known, was overshadowed by its more powerful neighbours. In comparison to the city-state of Tamassos, which grew rich from the nearby copper deposits, and Idalion with its Temple of Aphrodite, Ledra had little to commend it. In 280BC Leukos, the son of the Egyptian king Ptolemaios I, refounded the city and gave it his name, out of which the modern Greek name Lefkosia and the Turkish Lefkoşa have emerged. Why the French Crusaders named the town Nicosia is not clear.

When in the 7th century many of the islanders withdrew inland to escape the attacks of marauding Arabs, Nicosia became the capital. It enjoyed its greatest prosperity under the Lusignans (1192–1489), when the city became the residence of the Catholic archbishop and capital of the Crusader state of Cyprus. The population at that time was a colourful mixture: along with the Greek Orthodox majority and the Catholic feudal lords, there were Nestorians, Copts, Armenians and Jews. Wilhelm von Oldenburg, who visited the island as a pilgrim in 1210, compared the expansive and wealthy houses of Nicosia with the fine Crusader palaces of Antioch.

Venetian fortifications

A large palace, built in the 14th century, served as the seat of government for French nobles, but, like many other buildings, this fell victim to the Venetian military planners. Shortly before the Ottoman invasion, the Venetians (1489–1570) built a fortified wall around the city, and buildings situated in the field of fire were razed to the ground. Despite the wall, it only took two weeks for the Ottomans to overun Nicosia.

The 'Green Line'

In recent years, despite the many positive changes that have greatly reduced tensions and introduced freedom of movement across Cyprus's line of division, that border still exists and the underlying issues that produced it have yet to be resolved. The 'Green Line'still splits the old town of Nicosia in half. Abandoned houses, pockmarked with bullet holes, overlook this strip of no man's land that ranges from 10 to 30 metres in width. The asphalt surfaces are overgrown with grass, wild flowers and even young saplings, but they have nothing to do with the origin of the term 'Green Line'. The line was created with a green pen on a map in the UN peacekeeping mission's headquarters and marks the division between the Turkish Cypriot and Greek Cypriot sectors. Every now and then a UN patrol comprising soldiers in combat uniform and displaying the distinctive blue flag checks that the Greek Cypriot and Turkish troops sheltering behind the barbed wire have not changed the position of their sandbags or dug-outs – everything must remain exactly as it was at the time of the cease-fire. In an old car showroom, 'new' cars dating from 1974 lie buried beneath a thick layer of dust. The tranquillity is broken only when Greek and Turkish Cypriots take it in turns every few months to cut the grass and maintain the shrubs in the prohibited strip. But now, for the first time since 1974, there are real grounds for optimism that the Green Line might in time be dissolved and the city once more united.

At the Green Line

The Ömeriye Mosque

Shopping in Laïki Geitonia

Sights in the Southern Sector

The old town straddling the Green Line is the only part of Nicosia where places of historic interest and intriguing, narrow alleys are found.

Laïki Geitonia ❶, a delightful corner between Hippokrates Street and the D'Avila Bastion, is perhaps the highlight of the city's renovation programme. Street cafés, *tavernas* and souvenir shops attract visitors, although many of the houses are not quite as old as they look. They were rebuilt fairly recently in 1920s style.

The ★ **Leventis Municipal Museum** ❷ (Tuesday to Sunday 10am–4.30pm; free) documents the history of the city. A tour of the well-designed and large-scale exhibits provides an interesting insight into how the people of Nicosia used to live. The European Council awarded this museum the European Museum Prize for its bold, modern approach.

Hadji Georgakis Kornesios Mansion

The **Ömeriye Mosque** ❸ is the only Muslim house of prayer to have remained open in the Greek Cypriot section of the city. The original church that stood here was built in the Middle Ages for an Augustinian order and dedicated to John de Montfort who died here while participating in the Fourth Crusade in 1249. The church was destroyed by Mustafa Paşa during the Ottoman Conquest and a mosque dedicated to the prophet Omar was erected on the site. There is a fine view from the minaret.

The **Hadji Georgakis Kornesios Mansion** ❹ (Monday to Friday 8am–2pm, Saturday 9am–1pm; admission

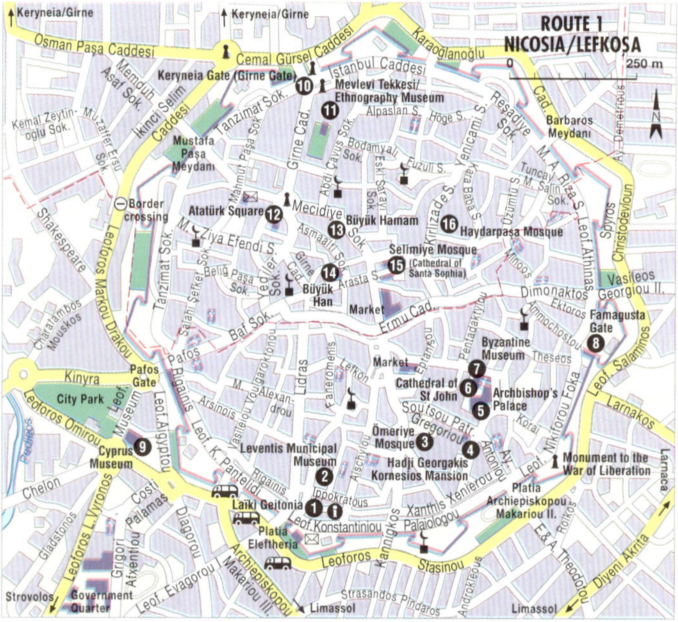

Inside the Cathedral of St John

charge) was erected in the 18th century and its interior clearly illustrates the opulent lifestyle of the upper strata of Ottoman society. The house was the residence of the dragoman (or interpreter) from 1779 to 1809. The holder of this post represented Cypriot Christians in their dealings with the Ottoman sultan and he was also responsible for collecting taxes for the Turkish rulers. His impressive possessions prove that he performed this task extremely well. On account of some intrigue, Georgakis Kornesios fell into disfavour and was beheaded in Constantinople in 1809.

The Archbishop's Palace

Outside the **Archbishop's Palace** ❺, built between 1956 and 1960, a huge bronze statue of Archbishop and President Makarios stands in solitary splendour. Facing him at the other end of the street is the **Monument to the War of Liberation**.

The Liberation Monument

The **Cathedral of St John** ❻ (Agios Ioannis; Monday to Friday 8am–noon and 2–6pm, Saturday 8am–noon) was built in 1662. Its modest exterior belies the splendour of its single-naved, barrel-vaulted interior. The iconostasis is covered with gold leaf and the colour of the 18th-century frescoes, only recently renovated, is of such a remarkable intensity that it would be easy to think that they had been completed only yesterday. Of special note is the series of pictures to the right of the bishop's throne. They show the discovery of the bones of St Barnabas and the subsequent recognition of the independence of the Cypriot church by the Byzantine emperor *(autokephalia)*.

More than 150 icons from all over Cyprus are displayed in the adjacent ★ **Byzantine Museum and Art Galleries** ❼ (Monday to Friday 9am–4.30pm, Saturday 8am– noon). The collection clearly illustrates the development of icon-painting from the 8th century up to the 18th century. Among the highlights of the museum are the Lythragkomi mosaics, which survived the attacks of the iconoclasts unscathed *(see*

Coffee break

Also seen on the £5 note

page 79). A number of 15th- to 19th-century European paintings with themes from Greek and Greek Cypriot history and mythology are displayed on the upper floor.

The nearby **Ethnographic Museum** (Monday to Friday 9am–1pm; admission charge) is housed in one of the city's oldest buildings, part of a former Benedictine monastery dating from the 15th century. On display here are costumes, everyday objects and equipment from before the industrial era. During the Lusignan period, the house belonged to the Benedictine monastery and later the Orthodox archbishop lived here.

The **Famagusta Gate** ❽, a replica of the Lazaretto Gate found in the wall at Heraklion (Crete), was the strongest section of the Venetian fortifications. The 35-m (115-ft) long barrel vaults and side chambers are now used for art exhibitions, conferences and lectures.

The 14 rooms of the ★ **Cyprus Museum** ❾ (Monday to Saturday 9am–5pm, Sunday 10am–1pm; admission charge) house the finest artefacts archaeologists have discovered on the island. Necklaces, small idols and items of pottery 6,000 years old from Choirokoitia bear witness to the fact that even in the Stone Age man understood about art and aesthetics. One such sculptor could not resist drawing attention to human weakness with humour. In the Bronze Age clay model of a mystery ceremony, a voyeur can be seen peering over the wall of the shrine. One showcase contains a selection of the 2,000 terracotta figures – some life-size – from Agia Irini (7th/6th century BC): warriors, priests with bull masks, minotaurs and sphinxes. Further highlights of the museum include the graceful 2-m (6-ft) high marble statue of Aphrodite of Soloi and the bronze figure of the Roman emperor Septimius Severus.

Just across the street from the museum are the welcome flowers, plants, trees, and shade of the **Municipal Gardens**.

The Famagusta Gate

Sights in Nicosia's Northern Sector: Lefkoşa

Keryneia Gate (Girne Gate) ⑩ was known in Venetian times as Porta del Provveditore and was the most northerly of the three gates in the town wall. This access point was closed in 1931 and the wall demolished on both sides to allow traffic to enter the old town from the north. The gate now stands forlornly on a traffic island, though it does house a tourist information office in summer.

Mevlevi Tekkesi/Ethnography Museum ⑪ (Monday to Friday 8am–1pm and 2–5pm) occupies a 17th-century Dervish monastery *(tekke)*. The hall was used by 'whirling dervish' monks who performed a long spinning dance until they reached a trance-like state. The practice was banned by Atatürk in 1925. Former monastery dignitaries are buried in the adjoining mausoleum.

Atatürk Square ⑫, now a pedestrian precinct and instantly recognisable from the metal bust of the founder of modern-day Turkey on one of the rooftops, was the secular centre of old Nicosia. Venetian and Ottoman governors lived in the Palazzo del Governo, which was demolished in 1904. The grey granite column in the middle of the square has travelled far. It originated in Egypt and was brought to Salamis by the Romans and incorporated into a temple. The Venetians dragged it to Nicosia in 1570 and crowned it with a lion as a symbol of Venice.

The ★ **Büyük Hamam** ⑬, or Turkish baths, predates the Ottoman era – it was probably once a church. The entrance, a replica of the portal of the monastic church at Acheiropoiitos, near Karavas (Alsancak), now lies at least 1m (3ft) beneath street level, as the adjacent houses and alleys were built on the rubble that had accumulated over the centuries.

★ **Büyük Han** ⑭ was once a caravanserai or a hostel for travellers. When restoration work is complete, it will become an art museum. A huge gate secured the inner courtyard, which served as both a marketplace and a pen for the travellers' camels and beasts of burden.

The Catholic Archbishop Thierry laid the foundation stone for the **Cathedral of Santa Sophia** ⑮ in 1209, but it is now the **Selimiye Mosque**. The building work lasted into the 14th century; in 1347 a papal bull was issued granting all the stonemasons a 100-day special indulgence. The west front with its three portals and large rose window is regarded as a masterpiece of French Gothic architecture. Moslems later removed all the fittings and Christian symbolism and painted the interior in plain white, adding to the dignity and elegance of the structure. The minaret offers a fine view of the town.

After serving as a church, mosque, register office, warehouse and sports hall, the **Haydarpaşa Mosque** ⑯, the second Gothic church in the city, is now an art gallery.

A quiet corner

Inside the Selimiye Mosque

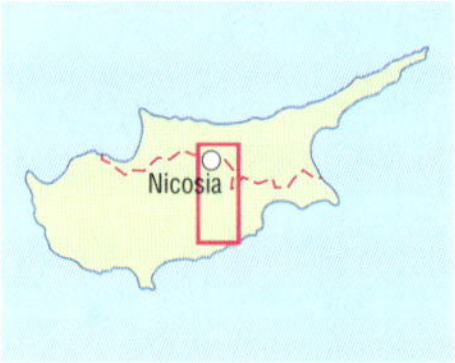

Route 2

The Mountain of the Cross and the village of lace

Nicosia – Lefkara (75km/46 miles)

The countryside near Pyrga

A hire car is advisable for this trip, which can easily be fitted into a day. The motorway out of Nicosia quickly leaves behind the city's business parks and industrial estates. First stop is the tiny village of Pyrga and its chapel of St Catherine, which echoes with the end of Frankish rule. Cyprus's oldest monastery crowns Stavrovouni, the Mountain of the Cross. From the summit the view over the wooded slopes of the neighbouring hills unfolds like a faded panoramic map, extending through the haze as far as the sea and the foothills of the Troodos. Between the two lies Lefkara where, since Venetian times, world-renowned lace has been made.

The unassuming **Agia Ekaterina** (St Catherine's) chapel

at **Pyrga** (daylight hours only, key from the *kafenion*; admission charge) was completed in 1421 during the latter years of Frankish rule and so symbolises the end of a dynasty that in its heyday was wealthy enough to endow the superb Gothic cathedrals of Nicosia and Famagusta and also Bellapais Monastery. As its power and wealth drained away, it could only afford to build this modest chapel, which is also known as the Chapelle Royale (Royal Chapel). In a stylistic sense, most of the frescoes are firmly in the Byzantine tradition. However, one or two figures, such as Maria Hodegetria (the 'Guiding Light') with the baby Jesus in her arms, betray the fact that the unknown painter was familiar with the art of the Italian Renaissance.

Visible in the lower section of the Crucifixion above the altar are a crowned couple, kneeling deep in prayer: King Janus de Lusignan (1398–1432) and Charlotte de Bourbon, his second wife. The chapel had belonged to the royal estate of Casal Piria, and it may be that the two were

St Catherine's chapel

Inside St Catherine's chapel

praying for God's help on 6 July 1426, the eve of the Battle of Choirokoitia in which the Lusignans were defeated by the Egyptian Mamelukes. The unfortunate Janus, who had already spent part of his childhood in a Genoese prison, was taken hostage and sent to Cairo. A year later he was released, after the Pope and other European courts raised the huge ransom of 200,000 ducats. But Janus, more popular than any other Catholic ruler of Cyprus, was broken.

Stavrovouni monastery

★ **Stavrovouni** (April to August daily 8am–noon and 3–6pm; September to March daily 8am–noon and 2–5pm; free, but donation appreciated) is the oldest monastery in Cyprus. Over the centuries a sacred relic, a fragment of the Cross, has attracted pilgrims to the monastery, which is perched on a prominent rock at 688m (2,255ft) and reached via a footpath from **Agia Varvara**.

The monastery was founded in 327 by the Empress Helena, the mother of Constantine the Great, on the site of a former Temple of Aphrodite – but women are not allowed in. The diary of Willibrand von Oldenburg who visited Cyprus in the 13th century explains why Helena brought the fragment of the cross from Jerusalem to Stavrovouni. According to the German pilgrim, 'the devil was continually tormenting the inhabitants. He pulled the newly buried from their graves at night and took them to the homes of his friends, so the people no longer wished to bury their dead. The understanding Helena brought the cross from Jerusalem to the mountain to drive the demons not just out of the area but also from the whole of the lower atmosphere'.

Quite apart from the relic, the reward for driving up to the top is the superb view.

Making lace in Lefkara

★ **Lefkara** is famous for the lace and embroidery the women have been making since the Venetians ruled the island. As early as 1481 Leonardo da Vinci obtained an altar cover here for Milan Cathedral. The geometric patterns and the finely-worked edging of the *lefkaritika* are a fusion of Greek, Byzantine and Venetian motifs. While their wares may strike some as expensive, it should be borne in mind that one tablecloth can take several weeks to produce. Lefkara is also noted for its silversmiths, and the 700-year-old cross at Tou Timiou Stavrou church stands as proof of the ability of the local craftsmen.

The Venetians appreciated the cooler summers of Lefkara, and the Italian influences on the church tower in the upper town are obvious. The houses are grand, and are reminiscent of the mountain hideaways of inland Sicily. The **village museum** (Monday to Thursday 9.30am–4pm, Saturday 10am–4pm; admission charge) in the extravagantly restored Patsalos House testifies to the considerable wealth of past years.

Route 3

Tamassos landscape

Monasteries and royal tombs *See map on pages 22–3*

Nicosia – Machairas – Fikardou (50km/31 miles)

This day trip starts at the cave church of the Virgin Mary, a genuine, popular shrine, complete with superstitions. Reaching Machairas monastery requires a long drive up through pretty wooded hillsides. An impressive monument to the freedom fighter Grigoriou Afxentiou, who died in battle against the British, gives the visitor an insight into the political role of the church. For those who have made the journey here by taxi rather than hire car, the return walk through the Pedieios valley to the Irakleidios convent and the royal tombs of Tamassos will take about half a day. A drive up the long winding road to Fikardou is well worth the effort: the open-air museum reveals the travails of life in the mountains.

Rural lifestyle

The cave church of Panagia Chrysospiliotissa in **Kato Deftera** is an ancient shrine, possibly dating back to the Bronze Age when an Asia Minor mother god was worshipped here. Popular belief ascribes the four man-made caves in the steep rock face above the Pedieios to the Virgin Mary: she is said to have scraped out the rock with her fingernails after the death of Christ so that she could grieve over the loss of her son in peace. Young women who come here to pray for a happy and fertile marriage have left unusual, touching offerings. Women hoping to conceive present wax limbs or whole wax babies, while those waiting for the right man to come along leave wedding veils and tiaras.

The barren region surrounding ancient **Tamassos** still bears the scars left by Bronze Age miners who dug for copper here over 3,500 years ago. They cut down the wood for fuel to melt the ore and left the slag piled up in enormous heaps, where even now only a few wild plants grow. Very little of the old town has been uncovered, apart from the foundations of a temple and some workshops. Unlike the tombs at Salamis *(see page 72)*, the entrances *(dromoi)* to the **Royal Tombs** (Tuesday to Friday 9am–3pm, weekends 10am–3pm), both of which date from between 650 and 600BC, take the form of steep flights of steps. The stone roof beams, false doors, window balustrades and frieze are modelled on wooden houses, similar to those in the Near East.

Agios Irakleidios

On the outskirts of Politiko, the **Agios Irakleidios** monastery stands above the grave of the eponymous murdered saint. The premises were abandoned many years ago but, on the initiative of Archbishop Makarios, a community of nuns was invited to make use of the restored buildings. They have created an enchanting garden, sell delicious honey and home-made confectionery and also watch over the gilded skull of the saint, who was a companion of St Paul. Visiting times are limited, and for group visits only.

Machairas

A narrow road winds its way through the wooded eastern foothills of the Troodos mountains to the ★★ **Machairas Monastery** (750m/2,460ft), situated in a stunning location beneath Mt Kionia. It is a popular destination for day-trippers and tourists alike, not least because of the shade and cooling breezes. The seasonal River Pedieios, which flows sluggishly through the plain, babbles cheerfully here. Outside the monastery, often

shrouded in mist during the winter, a *taverna* serves lamb braised in a clay oven and also a strong *eau-de-vie*.

A modern mosaic near the church door recounts the story of the 'Monastery of the Knife'. In the 12th century two hermits, Neophytos and Ignatios, stumbled upon a buried icon of the Virgin Mary guarded by a knife. According to another version, a dagger was actually thrust through the icon; a third, more prosaic theory suggests that the name derives from the wind which has a sharp cutting edge up here. Whatever the truth, the emperor Manuel I Comnenus (1143–80) presented the brethren with a considerable sum of money and large tracts of land to support the monastery. The early buildings have long since disappeared, as fire has ravaged the monastery on more than one occasion, most recently in 1892.

Machairas mosaic

The undisputed hero of the monastery is not, however, a devout man of the church, but a secular rebel. A small museum in the monastery remembers the exploits of the EOKA (National Organization of Cypriot Fighters) leader Grigori Afxentiou, and a monumental bronze figure of the Cypriot hero surveys the valley. In March 1957, during the struggle for independence, he was tracked down by British soldiers to a hide-out in a cave just below the monastery. He put up bitter resistance but was killed when his pursuers, angered by the death of one of their comrades, set his refuge on fire with a flame-thrower. The spot where Afxentiou died is decorated with wreaths and the Greek flag, and has been an important place of pilgrimage ever since.

Walkers can choose to take a taxi to Machairas and then enjoy a three-hour walk back down to the Irakleidios monastery on a rarely used track through the delightful Pedieios valley.

Fikardou

The lure of jobs in the towns has almost emptied the mountain village of ★ **Fikardou**, and now only a few elderly residents remain. However, it has been declared a site of historic interest, mainly for its 18th- and 19th-century rural-style houses.

While many of the houses may look as though they have been abandoned, some are still used. The dwellings have been faithfully restored, including the **Houses of Katsinioros and Achillea Dimitri**. Exhibits in this museum of rural life include old furniture, a grape press, a loom and a spinning wheel (May to September Tuesday to Friday 9am–4.30pm, Saturday 9am–4pm, Sunday 10am–1.30pm; October to April Tuesday to Friday 9am–4pm, Saturday 9am–3.30pm, Sunday 10.30am–2pm; admission charge). A guardian keeps an eye on things and looks after the key.

To return to Nicosia, take the shorter and quicker route on the E904 and E903.

Chapel of Asinou

A local priest

Route 4

Barn churches in the Troodos *See map on pages 22–3*

Nicosia – Limassol (180km/111 miles)

This tour, for which a hire car is essential, includes five of the most important churches in Cyprus. All have been granted the coveted World Cultural Heritage status by UNESCO. Because of their overhanging roofs they have been termed 'barn churches'. The valuable paintings inside retell not just events from the Old and New Testament which are important to the Eastern church but also the lives of the saints. There are some fine walks through the Troodos woodland from all the churches, and it would be a pity to have to restrict this route to just one day. Simply asking the priest for the key can often lead to some unexpected invitations from the friendly and hospitable villagers, and time can then pass very quickly.

The chapel at ★★ **Asinou** (daily 9am–5pm, until 4pm in winter; free but donation appreciated) stands in a lonely wooded spot above Nikitari, and the key may be obtained from the village priest. All the other monastery buildings which were part of the Panagia Forviotissa (1105) have long since disappeared, and likewise nothing remains of Arsine, which was mentioned by ancient writers and from which the name of the chapel derives.

Externally, the building has an unusual structure, mainly because of the steep, double pitch roof – hence the description 'barn church'. In fact the roof is typical of Troodos churches. On closer inspection it turns out to be an outer skin, which covers the domes and the barrel vaulting, a contrivance designed to protect **Panagia Forviotissa** from the elements. It is possible to tell from the picture of the founder above the south door that the barn roof was not a later addition but formed part of the original church. The narthex was added in 1200.

The true splendour of the church is evident from the interior: practically every square inch of the wall is covered with frescoes. After some very thorough cleaning and restoration work they now look as though they were finished yesterday. Most of the pictures date from the church's construction, with the more recent narthex painted in the 13th century. Some scenes were overpainted in 1333 and new motifs added. Faded paint was also touched up in the 16th century. No museum could better illustrate the development of Byzantine church painting. Simply compare the awe-inspiring and entranced Jesus in the resurrection scene in the sanctuary with the image created 200 years later in the porch where he looks benevolently down from the dome.

Perhaps the most impressive scenes are found in the rear, left-hand corner. The *Forty Martyrs of Sebasteia* shows 40 scantily clad, badly bleeding Christians, shivering on a frozen lake guarded by Roman legionaries. One of them can no longer withstand the torture and creeps off to the steaming bathhouse on the shore which is open to those who renounce their beliefs. But the place of the deserter is immediately taken by one of the guards.

★★ **Kakopetria** (671m/2,200ft), meaning 'useless rock', lies at the upper entrance to the Solea valley close to the village of **Galata**. Given the mild climate and the delightful surrounding countryside where fruit orchards, walnut trees and fertile gardens flourish by the banks of the Karyotis river, it is no surprise that even in Lusignan times both these villages were popular refuges from the lowland summer heat. Late medieval murals can be found in three churches here and all warrant closer inspection.

Troodos colour and landscape

The ★ **centre** of Kakopetria is an official site of historic interest. A circuit of the narrow ridge which is hemmed in by two streams is now firmly on the itinerary of all Troodos bus tours. At weekends in particular, the cobbled lanes resemble a bazaar with old women and children selling knitwear, honey and fruit. Green walnuts pickled in syrup is just one local speciality. Most of the houses were built in the 18th and 19th centuries from natural stone, wood and clay bricks.

Situated at the entrance to Galata is the church of ★ **Panagia tis Podythou** (also known as Eleousa, meaning 'the merciful'; open irregularly; free but donation appreciated), which was founded in 1502. The pictures here are thematically in the Byzantine tradition, but stylistically the influence of the Italian Renaissance is unmistakable. The unknown artist has given the lively figures portraitlike facial features and has emphasised the illusion of depth, a device quite alien to Byzantine art.

The frescoes in the nearby ★ **Panagia Theotokos** (also known as Agios Archangelos; 1514; open irregularly; free but donation appreciated) also show an interesting combination of East and West. To obtain the key, ask for the priest at the Louxis Pub by the bridge in Galata (not before 11am).

The ★★ **Agios Nikolaos tis Stegis** (St Nicholas of the Roof; Tuesday to Saturday 9am–4pm, Sunday 11am–4pm; free but donation appreciated) monastery church lies 5km (3 miles) to the southwest of Kakopetria (Tuesday to Saturday 9am–4pm, Sunday 10.30am–4pm). It was originally a domed cruciform basilica (11th century) which later acquired a saddleback roof and a narthex. In any beauty contest between the barn churches, Agios Nikolaos would win no prizes, especially when viewed from the outside. The extensions and alterations do not create a harmonious whole, but seem like the separate elements of a stage-set. However, an admirer of Cypriot church paintings may come to a different conclusion about the church. The frescoes in court style from the early Comnenian era (12th century), including, again, the *Forty Martyrs of Sebasteia*, surpass the Asinou frescoes in both elegance and craftsmanship.

A member of the congregation

A new panorama opens up

The **Pitsylia** region in the southeastern corner of the Troodos is one of the poorest parts of southern Cyprus. Mountain folds and running water have cut deep valleys out of the rock. Many of the settlements that cling to the hillsides are within hailing distance of each other but separated by a gruelling stretch of road across the valley.

Few people remaining in the region's 50 or so villages now devote their energies to wine production, once an important source of income. Cultivating the tiny terraces which are inaccessible to machinery is a backbreaking task and most of the working population prefer to get up early and drive to Nicosia or Limassol, if they have not already made the move to the towns. The Pitsylia Rural Development Project involves the construction of new irrigation systems and roads, the re-allocation of land, and financial assistance for farmers. But it has only slowed down the drift to the towns, not stopped it altogether.

Even in Pitsylia, walkers and art-lovers will find plenty to interest them. At the northern end of **Lagoudera** (1,000m/3,250ft), the ★★ **Panagia tou Araka** church (1192; daily 10am–4pm; free but donation appreciated) is all that remains of the estate of a wealthy Byzantine. The artist Leon Authentou, whose name is mentioned on an inscription in the church, was a skilful practitioner and he bequeathed some magnificent wall paintings. It would be hard to find figures portrayed so gracefully and movingly anywhere else on Cyprus. The care demonstrated by Authentou in the execution of the faces shows clearly that he had many years' training in the skills of icon-painting, probably in Constantinople. These wall paintings are genuine frescoes, that is to say the paint was applied to the still damp plaster – a painstaking task as the artist has to work a square inch at a time and every section must be completed in a few minutes, before the chalk dries. The painters who worked in other churches were less inclined to exercise such care. They worked on one picture at a time or covered a wider surface area, applying paint to an already dry background.

Perhaps Philip Goul, who painted the interior of the remote church of ★ **Stavros tou Agiasmati** (near Platanistasa; open irregularly; free but donation appreciated) around 1500, was familiar with the work of his more illustrious colleague, Authentou. Goul was a child of the Renaissance. He has used perspective particularly effectively in his foot-washing scene, his buildings look Italian in style, and he took the liberty of portraying scenes which were outside the repertoire of Orthodox iconography. A 10-part cycle in an arch in the north wall shows the Discovery of the Cross, a favourite theme not just for the Crusaders but also, given the relic of Stavrovouni *(see page 24)*, important for Cyprus too. The key is available from the priest in Platanistasa.

Backtracking, then taking the road through Platanistasa some 10km (6 miles) east to Palaichori, brings you to the latest of Cyprus's 10 UNESCO-recognised Troodos churches: **Metamorfosis tou Sotiros** (Transfiguration of the Saviour; open irregularly; free but donation appreciated), which dates from the early 16th century. Pride of place among the suite of interior frescoes in this steep-roofed church goes to a fine representation of the transfiguration of Christ, and of Cyprus's own St Mamas of Morfou riding on a lion.

Continue on to Limassol via Troodos and Pano Platres.

Panagia tou Araka

Inside Stavros tou Agiasmati

Christ the Pantocrator

Route 5

Visitors to Limassol castle

★ Limassol (Lemesos) – where tourism and trade rule

The second-biggest town in Cyprus, known in Greek as 'Lemesos', lies in the middle of the south coast. With its central location it is an ideal base for tourists wishing to make day trips. The wine festival in September, the carnival in spring and the range of evening entertainment at Potamos Germasogeias have given the 165,000 inhabitants a fun-loving reputation. But Limassol has changed since the Turkish invasion, and some detractors have accused the townspeople of profiting from the war. Despite the withdrawal of the Turkish community, some 45,000 refugees boosted the population dramatically. The port has certainly benefited from the Turkish occupation and has taken over from Famagusta as the main outlet for exports. The political problems in Lebanon also helped Limassol

as many members of Beirut's business community moved here in order to continue trading.

Unbridled growth has done little to improve the townscape. A belt of concrete, known to locals as 'The Wall', separates the town centre from the newly built promenade. The modern shopping streets have nothing special to offer and, as a consequence of the 1584 earthquake, there are few historic buildings to see. Only the bazaar around the Greek market hall and the Palaia Geitonia, the old Turkish quarter near the castle and mosque, are worth exploring. Most hotels overlook the narrow, sandy beach to the east of the town that extends for 15km (9 miles) as far as the ruins of Amathus *(see page 35)*.

Limassol harbour and fisherman

History

Burial finds within the town prove that a settlement existed here in the second millennium BC, but Nemesos, as it was known in antiquity, was overshadowed by the neighbouring cities of Amathus and Kourion. As early as the 6th century AD, Nemesos was the seat of a bishop, but it was the Crusaders who raised the town's status. Richard the Lionheart landed here on his way to the Holy Land and while based in Limassol he conquered the whole island. In Limassol castle on 12 May 1191 he married Berengeria, whose abduction by the Cypriot ruler Isaac Comnenos had initially led to the Crusaders' invasion. In 1291 Cyprus passed to the Knights Templar who ruled from Limassol, and later the Knights of St John administered their lands from here. But earthquakes, and attacks by the Genoese, Mamelukes and Ottomans brought the town to its knees. The English traveller William Turner, who visited the island in 1815, saw 150 mud huts here and described it as a 'pitiful place'. However, when the British decided to build a naval base here well over a hundred years ago, the town awoke from its slumber.

The castle gate

Inside Limassol castle

Sights

The **castle** ❶ (Monday to Saturday 9am–5pm, Sunday 10am–1pm; admission charge) is the only real historic site in the old town. The present building was constructed at the beginning of the 14th century over the ruins of an earlier Byzantine castle, which itself had a long and varied history. It was here that Richard I (the Lionheart) married Berengaria of Navarre and that Berengaria was subsequently crowned Queen of England by the Bishop of Evreux. From 1291 the castle belonged to the Knights Templar until this order was disbanded in 1308. King Janus handed the new citadel to the Knights of St John. In 1570, the Turks moved in and, later, the British used it as a prison.

The **Cyprus Medieval Museum** is housed in the vaults where gravestones, weapons, armour and other finds are displayed. The most spectacular exhibits are the three silver plates, discovered among the famous Lambousa Treasure in 1902, showing scenes from the youth of King David. Large-scale photographs introduce visitors to other medieval castles and churches on the island.

Although the best finds from the Limassol region are kept in the Cyprus Museum in Nicosia *(see page 20)*, several exhibits in the **Archaeological Museum** ❷ (Monday to Friday 10am–5pm, Saturday 10am–1pm; admission charge) deserve special attention. These include some expressive terracotta figures kneading bread dough, and a plump terracotta woman with a basket. The statue of Bes, an Egyptian-Mesopotamian god, was excavated in Amathus in 1978.

The castle battlements

When the stands are taken down at the end of the wine festival in Limassol's **municipal park**, the lions, monkeys and birds in Cyprus's only **zoo** ❸ become the town's main attraction. This is one of few places where it is possible to get a close-up view of moufflons, an extremely timid breed of wild sheep rarely seen in a natural setting. Some visitors to the zoo may be distressed by the inadequate conditions in which the animals are kept.

Welcome to the brewery

The large wine cellars and the brewery play their part in maintaining Limassol's reputation for cordiality. Based at the western end of the town on the way to the harbour, some firms provide guided tours and also opportunities to sample their products. For details of the rather irregular opening times, ask in a hotel or at the tourist information office.

A narrow sandy strip in front of the hotels at the eastern end of the town is popular with watersports enthusiasts, but the Lady's Mile Beach, protected by breakwaters at the western end of the town, is better. This beach lies within the confines of the British military base and passports may be requested.

Konnos Bay, Cape Gkreko

Route 6

The finest beaches *See map on pages 22–3*

Limassol – Agia Napa – Paralimni (110km/68 miles)

Holidaymakers based in Limassol who would like to sample other (better) beaches should try those in the far south-east of the island. Formerly shunned for its barren soil and sometimes mocked as the 'potato patch', after partition the region around Agia Napa, Protaras and Paralimni became for a time the most important tourist region. There is no doubt that this corner of Cyprus possesses the finest beaches, but despite the fine yellow sand, it also has concrete hotel blocks and other architectural monstrosities. And yet there are a few idyllic spots, such as the unspoilt and windswept Cape Gkreko or the fishing port of Potamos. From Deryneia, it is possible to peer across the demarcation line into the ghost town of Varosha (Maraş), now out of bounds even to Turkish civilians. The cultural highlights are the town of Larnaka *(see page 38)* and the Stone Age settlement of Choirokoitia. A hire car will be needed for these visits.

Touring by boat

The hotel quarter in Limassol has seen unbridled growth in recent years and now extends to the edge of the Hellenistic-Roman ruins at **Amathus**. In the 19th century all the larger stones were transported to Egypt for use in the Suez Canal, and today only the foundations remain. More recently, the Temple of Aphrodite on the acropolis has been partly restored and now offers a photogenic backdrop as the sun sets behind the sea of houses.

Governor's Bay, whose beauty derives from the bizarrely formed, white sandstone cliffs and the tiny, secluded coves, sometimes no more than a niche in the rock, ranks as one of the finest beaches on the south coast. *Tavernas* offer snacks and reasonably priced meals, and a large and well-maintained campsite offers overnight accommodation. At the moment there are few shaded pitches.

The Neolithic settlement of ★ **Choirokoitia** (September to March daily 9am–5pm; April to August Monday to Friday 9am–7.30pm, weekends 9am–5pm; admission charge) lies on the hillside above the River Maroni. The walls of the round, stone huts *(tholoi)* date from the 7th millennium BC and for many years were thought to be the oldest traces of life on the island, but archaeologists at Kalavassos (Kastros) have found a village even older, and at Cape Gata a store dates from the Middle Stone Age.

Neolithic Choirokoitia

The lines of foundations are confusing, with the remains of settlements centuries apart lying on top of each other. By 3800BC Choirokoitia had been abandoned for good. Finds reflect the advances in human development. The first inhabitants lived from fishing and hunting and only with time did they learn how to sow fields with cereals and pulses, and to breed livestock. Sometimes it was immigrants from Syria and Cilicia who brought these new skills.

As for tools, sharp spear tips made from obsidian have been found; but this lava rock does not occur on Cyprus, so Stone Age man in Choirokoitia must have had trading links with the mainland. The way in which the round huts were built is best seen from the *tholos* close to the entrance. Two pillars supported a false wooden ceiling and on the outside a kind of canopy surrounded the huts. Archaeologists dispute whether the reconstruction displayed in Nicosia's Cyprus Museum *(see page 20)* is accurate. The dead were buried beneath the house with a heavy stone laid on their chest to prevent their return. Clearly the relationship between the generations even then was not always plain sailing.

Agia Napa monastery

Once a peaceful fishing village, **Agia Napa** promises sun and fun and is almost totally dependent on tourism. The 400-year-old **monastery** in the town centre provides a conference centre for the World Council of Churches. Its most attractive features are the Venetian fountain in the courtyard and the chapel. At the town hall on Odos Agia Mavris is the small **Tornaritis-Pierides Marine Life Museum** (Monday to Friday 9am–2pm, Saturday 9am–1pm; admission charge), which has a collection of seashells and stuffed or preserved fish and other sea creatures.

But nobody comes to Agia Napa for peace and quiet. Fine yellow sand, windsurfing and boat hire, riding and diving make it an ideal resort for watersports enthusiasts, while in Nissi Bay pelicans keep the children entertained. Such sedate attractions can't disguise the fact that Agia Napa is a sun-sea-and-sand destination, nor that the fourth S-word (sex) has taken centre-stage as the resort has emerged as one of the Mediterranean's hottest clubbing venues. The bars in Seferis Square are popular meeting places in the evening and the dance clubs stay open until dawn.

All aboard!

Night lights in Agia Napa

With its attractive rocky shore and inlets, **Cape Gkreko**, the southeastern tip of Cyprus, has been declared a nature conservation area. As well as many tourists, migratory birds visit the cape, pausing here before continuing their long journeys. For many of them, however, Cyprus turns out to be their last resting place as the local people cannot allow such delicacies to pass them by. The branches of the trees where the weary creatures sit are coated with birdlime and so for many of them the long trek south ends prematurely either in a Cypriot stew or on a barbecue.

Cape Gkreko

A 2-km (1¼-mile) walk leads round the karst rock. On foot the cape can be reached from Agia Napa in just under two hours but sections of the path cross rough terrain. There is no proper footpath along the east coast to **Protaras** and **Pernera** either. These last two beach resorts, which have grown up during the last few years, are close to the small town of **Paralimni**.

Once water was abundant here. Creaking wind pumps, a typical feature of the region, drew the water from below ground – it was even stored in a lake during the winter – and the farmers turned the reddish-brown soil into very fertile land. But intensive agriculture has caused the water table to sink ever lower and now electric pumps are required to draw the water from deep bore holes.

Deryneia has a Checkpoint Charlie atmosphere. As the last village before Famagusta, cafés and *tavernas* jockey for the best view of the 'occupied land' and the lost home of Greek Cypriot refugees.

Larnaka's old port

Route 7

★ Larnaka – boomtown behind the beach

With a population of 75,000, Larnaka is Cyprus's third-largest town and, after Limassol, is the most important port in the Greek Cypriot sector. The palms beside the promenade give a hint of Nice and Cannes and Mediterranean flair, and the sandy beach is ideal for sunbathing. In the adjoining marina, amateur sailors from all over the world meet and share their experiences.

A timeless occupation

Most holidaymakers fly into Larnaka, which became the island's principal airport when Nicosia airport was forced to close after the Turkish invasion. But Larnaka has kept a sense of normality. A walk through the former Turkish quarter around the mosque still has an Oriental feel, and the lively bazaar district near the Agios Lazaros church makes an interesting place for a stroll. The seemingly endless sandy beach in the east of the town is overlooked mainly by hotels.

History

According to legend, Kition, as Larnaka was known in antiquity, was founded by Kittim, one of Noah's grandsons. Whether that is true or not, archaeologists have found the remains of a settlement which dates from the 2nd millennium BC. In 1075BC the town was destroyed by an earthquake, but was rebuilt in the 8th century BC by the Phoenicians, for whom it was an important trading post. The town's most famous son is Zeno, born here in 336BC. He went on to found the Stoic school of philosophy in Athens. The Stoics believed that man should not be guided by feelings or lust but by reason. Zeno lived to old age, but then committed suicide.

The Lusignan name for Larnaka was Salina, after the nearby salt deposits, but the Genoese named it Scala or

'Port'. Today's name for the town was coined by the Venetians who during the Renaissance were interested primarily in the ancient ruins of Cyprus and gave the settlement the name Larnax (meaning 'stone sarcophagus').

Sights

The **Turkish fort** ❶ (Monday to Friday 9am–5pm; March to May until 6pm, June to August until 7pm, September to October until 6pm; admission charge), built in 1625, dominates the coastal skyline. Old cannons still stand on the huge walls. Inside, the castle displays archaeological finds from Kition and the Bronze Age settlement by the salt lake.

The church of **Agios Lazaros** ❷ (April to August daily 8am–12.30pm and 3.30–6.30pm; September to March daily 8am–12.30pm and 2.30–5pm; free) was built by the Byzantine emperor Leo VI (886–912) above the grave of the town's patron saint. According to legend, Lazarus, whom Christ raised from the dead, fled to Cyprus to escape from the Jews

The Church of Agios Lazaros

Inside Agios Lazaros

of Bethany. He later became the bishop of Kition. Emperor Leo discovered his tomb in 890 and sent the remains to Constantinople. They were later removed by Crusaders who took them to Marseilles. In 1970 a tomb with just a skull inside was discovered beneath the church. The skull was gilded and is on display. Visitors must decide for themselves if it ever sat on the shoulders of Lazarus. The English cemetery bears witness to that period in Cyprus's history when Larnaka was an important staging post on the Europe–Asia trade route.

The ★ **Pierides Museum** ❸ (Monday to Thursday 9am–4pm, Friday to Saturday 9am–1pm; admission charge) in Odos Zinonos Kitieos is well worth a visit. For over six generations the Pierides family collected antiquities and these are now displayed in this fine mid-18th-century mansion. The furnishings also give an insight into the lifestyle of wealthy Cypriots around the turn of the 19th century. Among the highlights are ceramics that range from the Early Stone Age to the Middle Ages.

The **Municipal Cultural Centre** ❹ houses a palaeontological exhibition (Tuesday to Friday 9am–2pm, Saturday and Sunday 9am–noon; admission charge), including skeletal remains of dinosaurs, the Cypriot dwarf hippopotamus, and temporary monthly exhibitions. Devotees of ancient history may well be interested in the **Archaeological Museum** ❺, the **Acropolis** ❻ and the **excavations of ancient Kition** ❼. At the latter site, archaeologists have uncovered the foundations of Mycenaean and Phoenician temples and workshops where copper implements were made.

Beaches stretch east and west

To avoid the crowds on the town beach, try Makenzie Beach or beaches near the hotels in the west of the town.

Hala Sultan Tekke

Excursions

Farmers no longer shovel salt from the salt lake in the southwest of the town, but during the winter it is visited by migratory birds, among them flamingos. Rising up from the bank in a well-tended garden is the minaret of the **Hala Sultan Tekke** (April to September daily 7.30am–7.30pm; October to March daily 9am–5pm; free but donation expected), the most important place of pilgrimage for Muslim Cypriots. Hala Sultan was a relative of the prophet Mohammed who came with an Arab army to the island in 649. According to legend, she fell from her mule, broke her neck and died here.

Apart from Thessaloniki in Greece and St Catherine's Monastery in the Sinai peninsula, the apse of ★ **Panagia Angeloktisti** (daily 8am–noon and 2–5pm; free but donation appreciated) in **Kiti** (11km/7 miles) is the only place in the eastern church where a mosaic (6th-century) dating from before the iconoclastic era *(see page 79)* has survived. Mary, flanked by the Archangels, stands on a jewelled footstool with the Christ child in her arms.

Route 8

On the trail of Aphrodite and Apollo

Limassol – Pafos (70km/43 miles)

To make the most of this route you need a car. The itinerary follows the coast to one of Cyprus's most significant ancient sites. Lush citrus groves, planted by Greek Cypriots evicted from Morfou, border the barren Akrotiri peninsula, and nearby lies the fortress of the Knights of St John at Kolossi. Situated on a plateau above the coastal plain, ancient Kourion is worth a visit, but then comes a difficult choice: whether to recover on the beach or continue on to Aphrodite's Rock where the goddess emerged from the sea. Conclude the journey with a visit to the Sanctuary of Aphrodite at Kouklia, often mentioned in the same breath as Olympia or Delphi.

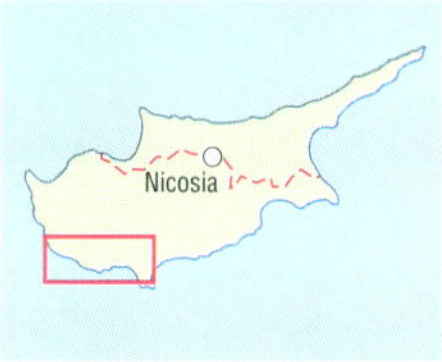

On the battlements at Kolossi

Kolossi Castle

The Knights of St John's ★ **Kolossi Castle** (September to May daily 9am–5pm; June to August daily 9am–7.30pm; admission charge) stands in a fertile region which from the 14th century supplied Europe with sugar and a sweet dessert wine known as Commandaria. Profits began to suffer later when the Venetians were driven out by the Ottomans and competition arrived in the form of cheap sugar from the New World. Gradually the Turks replaced sugar cane with cotton.

Before the Knights of St John settled on Rhodes, Kolossi was for a short time the headquarters of the famous order. The defensive tower house which has survived until today was constructed in the 15th century when the knights needed to fortify themselves against attacks from Mamelukes and Ottomans. Nearby stands a water-powered mill which crushed sugar cane. Water was diverted to Kolossi from the River Kouris across an aqueduct and then tumbled 11m (35ft) downhill through a narrowing channel. Juice squeezed from the cane was probably boiled in the hall with the distinctive barrel roof. The liquid was then poured into clay vessels where the sugar crystallised into a conical mass – sugarloaf.

Walk from the castle under the aqueduct of the old sugar mill and turn left at the next crossroads to arrive at the pilgrimage site of **Panagia Vounarkotissa**, a cave at the foot of a hill. The inside of the chapel is adorned with wax votive gifts, and in between them, as well as on the rocks next to the entrance, hang pieces of cloth, offerings through which the devout believe their wishes might be fulfilled.

A young theatregoer

The ruins of ★ **Kourion** (June to August daily 9am–7.30pm; September to May daily 9am–5pm; admission charge) stand on the cliff-tops against the background of an enchanting coastal landscape. After the mosaics of Pafos, these must rank as the most interesting excavations in the Greek Cypriot sector. A tour of the site can be combined with a swim in the Mediterranean. At the foot of the cliff lies a wide, sheltered bay with grey-brown sand.

Kourion, a city founded by Achaean colonists, flourished under Ptolemaic rule but, after attacks by Arab raiders in the 7th century, it was abandoned and the bishopric transferred to the more secure Episkopi.

The **Roman Theatre**, which had room for 3,500 spectators, has been restored and since 1963 it has staged both ancient and modern dramas. Given the fine acoustics of the sea-facing semi-circular amphitheatre, it has been used to make sound recordings. In antiquity, the theatre would have been covered by canvas and a stage wall as high as the top row of seats would have blocked the view out to sea, but over the centuries this complex of Hellenistic origins has been adapted to suit the requirements of the time.

Enjoying the acoustics

At the beginning of the 3rd century, new gangways were cut through the stand, the two front rows were removed and railings erected between the stage and auditorium: the theatre was then the scene for contests between gladiators and wild animals. A hundred years later, when audiences preferred watching traditional drama, the barriers were removed and the front rows rebuilt. After an earthquake in 365, the theatre was abandoned and the site dismantled.

Visitors to the adjoining **Villa of Eustolios** will be greeted in a passage by the timeless inscription 'Enter and bring good luck to the house'. Eustolios built this sumptuous peristyle residence with its superb mosaics in the early Christian period. He was probably not too sure about his own beliefs: Christian symbols such as fish and the plea for Christ's protection accompany an inscription addressed to Apollo.

Image of the Creation

The mosaic panels in the **baths** display not just birds, fish, and a partridge, but also a symbolic representation of the architect's skill: Ktisis, a personification of the Creation, holds a ruler the length of a Roman foot.

The early Christian basilica and adjacent episcopal palace lie at the northwestern edge of the site. Built around AD400 from recycled stone blocks, the church measured 37m x 55m (120ft x 180ft) and would have been of extravagant splendour in order to impress converts used to grandiose temples. On both sides of the three naves were additional halls from where the unbaptised could watch Mass. The narthex was also set aside for doubters. Anyone who wished to be baptised was immersed in the cross-shaped basin in the baptismal chapel to the north. The smaller basins were used for the ritual washing ceremony of the early Christians.

The Temple of Apollo Hylates

Unlike the Temple of Aphrodite in Old Pafos, which drew pilgrims from all over the ancient world, the **Sanctuary of Apollo Hylates** (June to August daily 9am–7.30pm; September to May daily 9am–5pm; admission charge) was of only regional significance. It lies on the main road behind the stadium 2km (1¼ miles) to the west of the basilica. From the 5th century BC onwards Apollo was worshipped as the protector of the woods and animals. The sanctuary had formerly been dedicated to an unknown goddess of fertility. The columns and facade, which give some indication of the size and splendour of the temple, have been rebuilt by archaeologists. The oldest and most interesting part of the sacred site is the tree sanctuary. Here seven holes through which sacred trees once grew have been cut in a circular rocky plateau 18m (59ft) in diameter, and a paved processional way leads around the site.

The waste pits near the shrine were of special interest to the excavating team. Analysis of the ashes revealed that animals, mainly lambs, had been sacrificed. When there was no more room in the temple for the pilgrims' votive offerings, the priests buried them. One pit contained many small clay figurines of animals or praying humans. The sale of these sacrificial and devotional gifts provided the priests with their livelihood.

Pissouri, halfway between Limassol and Pafos, has nothing of historic interest to offer, but it is a good place for an overnight stop or at least a rest. Situated on a 200m (650ft) high plateau between the coast road and the sea, the town centre is dominated by a huge rubber tree, where the old men congregate. British holidaymakers, in particular, appreciate the centre. Beach apartments and a luxury hotel by the bay are just under an hour's walk away.

The Rock of Aphrodite

★ **Petra tou Romiou**, literally the 'The Rock of Romios', but better known as the 'Rock of Aphrodite', is the most beautiful section of Cyprus's long coast. The bright white chalk contrasts with the azure blue sea, and the widely scattered rocks send spray high into the air. It was here that the beautiful Aphrodite 'born of sea foam' *(see*

page 77) emerged from the Mediterranean and set her delicate feet on Cypriot soil.

Only scanty remains have survived from the **Sanctuary of Aphrodite** (daily 9am–4pm; admission charge) near ★ **Kouklia** (Old Pafos). In contrast to the traditional temples, the sacred site for Aphrodite of Pafos was an open courtyard. The Cyclopean wall in the southwest corner is the shrine's oldest section, some of it dating from the Bronze Age. Many of the stones have been drilled through by peasants and bounty hunters in search of mythical treasure. The faithful in Old Pafos worshipped a mother god as long ago as the 2nd millennium BC, but the object of their devotion was a black, conical stone which is now displayed in the museum. She later became linked with the Babylonian-Phoenician Ishtar and finally Aphrodite. During the Roman era the sanctuary attracted pilgrims from all over the Mediterranean. Even emperors came to pay their respects.

Sanctuary of Aphrodite

Little is known about the mysterious ceremony with which the pilgrims invoked the blessings of the goddess. The participants were obliged to maintain absolute secrecy, and so much was left to the imagination. At the sacred ceremony, priests and priestesses are said to have copied the mythical union of Aphrodite and Kinyras, the founder of the shrine; at the same time priestesses gave themselves to the pilgrims. Herodotus draws a parallel between this type of ritual and temple prostitution. According to other reports, every girl from Pafos was obliged to visit the temple before her wedding and sleep with a stranger. Whatever the truth, the stories provided male pilgrims with an incentive to make the trip to Pafos.

The small **La Covocle** estate dates back to Lusignan times, although the gate was added by the Ottomans. Like Kolossi, it was the centre of a sugar plantation. The **museum** contains a few superbly presented and clearly described exhibits. Apart from the Aphrodite stone, the most striking item is a huge 2,000-year-old bath tub – without a drain hole. A model illustrates the Persian attack on Old Pafos in 498BC. The principal evidence for this archaeologists' reconstruction is a siege ramp that was found to the northeast of the village. The Persians showered the defenders with stones and then battered the city walls with a siege engine. The citizens of Pafos tried in vain to undermine the ramp with tunnels and to set the siege engine on fire.

Museum at La Covocle

At the edge of the site stands a partially uncovered Roman peristyle house. To the northwest a mosaic in the House of Leda shows Leda and the Swan surrounded by geometric patterns. In 1980 thieves dismantled and stole the mosaic but, miraculously, it was recovered. This mosaic is a replica and the original is now displayed in the Cyprus Museum in Nicosia *(see page 20)*.

Oleander adds colour

Turkish fort in Pafos

Route 9

★★★ Pafos – holiday resort among ruins and tombs

Visitors to western Cyprus might wonder why tourism did not arrive in this small town (pop. 50,000) until the 1980s. Bananas thrive in the mild climate on the artificially irrigated coastal plain, and the lower town, Kato Pafos, lies in the heart of one of Cyprus's most interesting archaeological zones. There are ancient and medieval ruins within this small area and every excavation yields new discoveries. Among the sights of historic interest are masses of hotels, souvenir shops and bars: since the opening of the nearby international airport, sleepy Pafos has become the boom town in the west, the focal point of a development splurge up and down the coast that verges on the frenetic.

Following the renovation of its old customs houses, most of them now *tavernas*, the harbour quarter has become an even more important attraction, while away from the seafront promenade, the town's bustling nightlife continues until well into the night. Many hotels occupy a good position overlooking the seafront.

The town is divided into two, with the upper town, Ktima, 3km (2 miles) from the sea (though urban sprawl has all but connected the two parts). Although modernising fast, its simple *tavernas* and basic shops can still just about evoke a sense of rural charm. The Classical-style complex of school, library and town hall near the municipal park dates from the era of British colonial rule.

Banana cultivation

A new friend

History

Despite its name, Nea Pafos (meaning New Pafos, so-called to avoid confusion with Palaia Pafos, or Old Pafos, the location of the Sanctuary of Aphrodite) the settlement here dates from ancient times. It is said to have been founded by King Agapenor after the Trojan War. Archaeologists believe that Nikokles, the last priest king of Old Pafos, built New Pafos about 320BC. With increasing numbers of pilgrims visiting the Shrine of Aphrodite, a larger port was thought to be necessary. Choosing the nearest point to the Egyptian port of Alexandria, the Ptolemaic rulers made New Pafos the island's administrative centre. The Roman governors also used Pafos as their capital and at that time it supported a population of some 30,000 – almost as many as live here today. Decline set in during late antiquity, but the Crusaders and Venetians still considered the town important enough to have a Catholic bishop. Francesco Contarini, the town's last senior cleric, was killed when Nicosia was captured by the Ottomans.

House of Dionysos, mosaic

Sights

The **fort** ❶ (June to August daily 10am–6pm; September to May daily 10am–5pm; admission charge), built by the Turks in 1592, overlooks the fishing harbour. Nearby lies a heap of stones left over from earlier fortifications which the Venetians destroyed in 1570 as they had too few soldiers to maintain a permanent guard.

Northwest of the harbour lay the centre of the Roman town. In 1962 a farmer ploughing his field chanced upon an ancient mosaic. Since then, archaeologists have uncovered further ★★★ **mosaics** (June to August daily 8am–7.30pm; September to May daily 8am–5pm; admission charge) in the vicinity and these now rank among the most significant and finest sights of historic interest in Cyprus. Even those visitors who do not find ancient ruins particularly appealing ought not to overlook these fascinating scenes from ancient mythology. Some of their tiny coloured blocks of stone were probably made in Alexandria in the 3rd and 4th centuries and shipped to Pafos before being assembled; others are of local origin. They are of such beauty and so well preserved that UNESCO has justifiably acclaimed the mosaics as a World Cultural Heritage site.

The owner of the ★★ **House of Dionysos** ❷ must have had a penchant for wine, as the god of wine, Dionysos, occupies a dominant position; hence the name that the archaeologists gave to this atrium villa. Liaisons illustrated on the mosaics include Pyramus and Thisbe, Zeus and Ganymede, Narcissus with his mirror image, and other couples. A series of hunting scenes and geometrical patterns complete the picture.

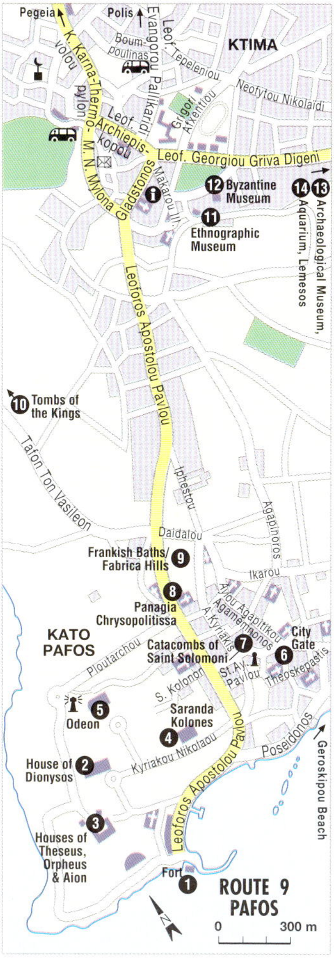

The Odeon – now open to the elements

Catacombs of St Solomoni

Polish archaeologists have been responsible for excavating the ★ **House of Theseus** ❸, probably the official residence of the Roman governor. Signs of Christian influence are already evident on the mosaic showing the birth and ablutions of Achilles. The round picture in the middle depicts the heroic Theseus as victor over the slain minotaur, while beneath it a man symbolises the scene of the triumph, the labyrinth, which also appears as a geometric pattern at the margin. Above, Ariadne is shown helping Theseus to make his way out of the maze by following the woollen thread.

The three mosaics in the **House of Orpheus** are stylistically close to those in the Dionysos villa. Here Orpheus charms wild animals with his music and Hercules wrestles with a lion. The mosaics in the **House of Aion**, laid after 342, show the birth, youth and triumphal procession of Dionysos. In terms of subject matter and the baroque shapeliness of the naked bodies, they are both in the ancient tradition, but here too similarities with the life of Christ cannot be overlooked. Archaeologists are still at work in the **House of the Four Seasons**, but it is hoped that the treasures unearthed here will soon be made accessible to the public.

The fortress of **Saranda Kolones** ❹ was built by the Byzantines from the remains of ancient buildings. An earthquake in 1222 destroyed the castle shortly after it had been reinforced by the Crusaders.

The **odeon** ❺ can still accommodate over 1,000 spectators and it regularly stages open-air concerts and plays. Only half of the 25 rows, built on the slopes of the acropolis in the 2nd century, have been restored, but today's audiences have to do without the roof that formerly offered some protection from summer sun and winter rain.

Northeast of the lighthouse, you can stroll along the top of the old city wall. From the **city gate** ❻ a ramp carved out of the rock leads down to the beach.

A huge terebinth tree casts its shadow over the steps to the **Catacombs of Saint Solomoni** ❼. Solomoni was forced to flee from Palestine in 168 and lived in this Hellenistic burial chamber. A spring in the base of the cave is said to cure eye complaints and anyone who ties a piece of material to the tree at the top is said to have their wish fulfilled as soon as the cloth starts to rot.

The simple 13th-century cruciform **Panagia Chrysopolitissa** ❽ basilica stands amid the remains of the 50 x 38m (160 x 125ft) five-naved early Christian **Agia Kyriaki** basilica. This was destroyed soon after the Crusaders arrived as they built a Gothic church nearby. However, the place was important for both Orthodox and Western Christians on account of **St Paul's Pillar**. According to legend, when Paul came to Cyprus on his first journey, he was arrested by Jews, tied to this pillar and whipped. The *Acts of the Apostles* makes no direct reference to this incident, but does recount (13, 4–12) that Paul blinded a sorcerer in Pafos, and the proconsul Sergius Paulus, who witnessed the event, was converted to Christianity. North of the pillar lie the **Frankish baths** ❾, the town's old bathhouse.

Other graves and underground chambers were carved out beneath **Fabrica Hill**, by the site of the Catacombs, and in the Middle Ages they housed a cotton mill. Couples may be interested in **Agios Agapetikos**, which is a rock chapel for lovers, sited on the hill's eastern flank. The **Digenis Rock** on the north side of the hill is the subject of a fascinating legend *(see page 77).*

The **Tombs of the Kings** ❿ (June to August daily 8am–7.30pm; September to May daily 8am–5pm; admission charge) are some distance away and best reached by bus or car. Buried here in lavish vaults hewn from the rock are not, in fact, kings, but the upper strata of Ptolemaic and Roman society. With Doric pillars surrounding an inner courtyard, some of these chambers replicate the villas of the living. Amid these monuments lie more modest catacombs and gravestones. When Christians were being persecuted, in antiquity and again during the Middle Ages, they sheltered in the cemetery.

Professor Georgios Elliades and his wife spent their lives collecting *objets d'art* and other everyday items belonging to farmers. These treasures are now accessible to the public in the **Ethnographic Museum** ⓫ (Monday to Saturday 9.30am–5pm, Sunday 10am–noon; admission charge), which forms a part of their home. A house chapel constructed in an ancient rock tomb is also worth investigating.

Ethnographic Museum exhibits

Icons from the 12th–18th century, liturgical objects and finely embroidered vestments are displayed in the **Byzantine Museum** ⓬ (April to October Monday to

Friday 9am–5pm, Saturday 9am–1pm; November to March Monday to Friday 9am–4pm, Saturday 9am–1pm; admission charge) housed in the bishop's residence.

The artefacts on show in the four rooms of the **Archaeological Museum** ⓭ (Monday to Friday 7.30am–5pm, until 6pm on Thursday, weekends 10am–1pm) are arranged in chronological order ranging from Early Stone Age burial offerings found in Lempa to a Renaissance baldachin. One extraordinary find is a set of clay hot-water bottles fashioned to fit the shape of a human body. They were probably made for treating a Roman dignitary who had rheumatism.

A good attraction for children is the **aquarium** ⓮ (daily 10am–8pm; admission charge) which displays colourful tropical fish from around the world.

To find a decent beach, you need to go to Geroskipou beach at the southern end of the Pafos seafront, or take the bus up the coast to either of the beaches at Coral Bay *(see page 54)*.

Geroskipou

Agia Paraskevi inside and out

Excursion

Geroskipou, on the road to Limassol, was formerly a separate village but is now a suburb of Pafos. The name means 'Sacred Grove' and it is said that pilgrims arriving at Pafos harbour rested here on their way to the Sanctuary of Aphrodite *(see page 45)*. However, little remains of this idyllic spot in a village which suffers badly from heavy traffic.

In addition to places selling its local speciality, *loukoumia*, a fruit jelly dusted with icing sugar for which Geroskipou is famous, there are two places of interest in the village. On the main square is ★ **Agia Paraskevi**, one of Cyprus's oldest churches. It has the usual Greek-cross ground plan, and is surmounted by five domes. When restoration work was carried out in the interior, simple wall paintings with geometric patterns and stylised flowers and crosses, typical of the iconoclastic period (728–843) were discovered underneath more recent frescoes. Hence the church must have been built in the 9th century at the latest. The positioning of the Blessed Virgin in the central dome is unusual; in the Byzantine tradition of church painting, Christ as Pantocrator occupies this position.

A **Folk Art Museum** (July to August Monday to Friday 7.30am–2.30pm; September to June Monday to Wednesday and Friday 9am–2.30pm, Thursday 9am–2.30pm and 3–6pm; admission charge), close by in the 200-year-old house of the consular agent Hadji Smith Zymboulakis, is a fine example of traditional village architecture. It contains not only the usual rural furniture and finely carved cabinets, the clothes and household objects of earlier generations, but demonstrates also the arts of domestic silk and cotton spinning and linen production.

Agios Neofytos monastery

Route 10

The wild west *See map on page 41*

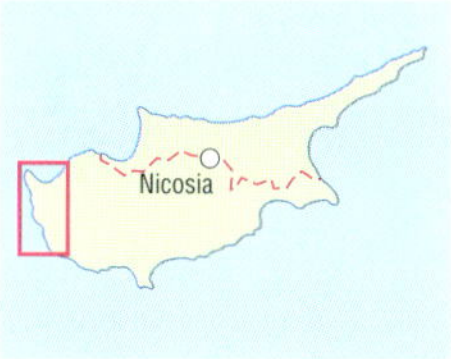

Pafos – Akamas peninsula (95km/59 miles)

The Akamas peninsula, a favourite haunt of nature-lovers, has been saved – for the time being at least – from property developers by environmental campaigners and so the turtle breeding ground at Lara beach remains undisturbed. Walkers can enjoy a day out in the Avgas Gorge and also the half-day nature trail near the 'Baths of Aphrodite'. The little town of Polis is popular with young independent travellers as it is one of the few places in Cyprus where overnight accommodation is available in small *pensions* or cheap private rooms. But Polis, like Pafos, is expanding fast. The full tour is best undertaken by car, but it is suitable for cyclists as long as they are not afraid of quite a few steep hills and energy-draining heat. Walkers will have to use taxis to reach the more remote sights as buses only operate between Pafos and Polis.

Ancient texts at Agios Neofytos

First stop is ★ **Agios Neofytos** monastery (April to October daily 9am–noon and 2–6pm; November to March daily 9am–4pm; monastery free, admission charge for sanctuary and museum). The story goes that St Neofytos, who had a love of travel, had been robbed of his money in Pafos in 1159 while en route to Palestine. Impoverished, he saw his plight as a sign from God and decided to stay put. The spot he chose for his enclosure *(enkleistra)*, where he was to spend the next 65 years, was by a spring at the entrance to a wooded valley.

Even during his lifetime, the walls of **Neofytos's cell**, smoothed with a layer of plaster, were covered with splendid paintings. Two of the scenes show Neofytos himself.

At the altar, Agios Neofytos

Neofytos's cells

In one he is being carried up to heaven by angels and in the other he is kneeling at the feet of Christ, flanked by John and Mary. In the **monastery church**, there are three clear styles. In the ascetic-style frescoes on the west wall, the saint, clad only in sack-like drapes, seems sullen and weary. The pictures in the apse of the chapel are quite different: the figures here display refinement and elegance and were the work of artists from the imperial court in Constantinople. The most recent pictures, such as the foot-washing scene, were added during restoration work in 1503 and the style has a more popular appeal.

Visitors to Agios Neofytos should also look inside the new **museum**. At weekends and on 28 September, St Neofytos's Day, the monastery is transformed into a busy market and it is difficult to imagine that once a hermit communed with God and nature here. For a hermit, however, Neofytos played an extraordinarily active part in the island's politics. Apart from a wealth of religious writings, he penned a chronicle entitled *Regarding the Misfortune of Cyprus*, a detailed account of the Crusaders' conquest of the island.

For a long time ★ **Polis** (pop 2,000) has been popular with young independent holidaymakers. There are few hotel complexes and visitors can stay in small pensions or private rooms rented out by locals. However, even in Polis Chrysochou, the 'Town with the Golden Sand' as it is officially known, there is an increasing number of hotels, villas and apartment blocks and the attractive main square and the street leading to the pedestrianised zone have been smartened up.

In antiquity, the town of Marion/Arsinoë was a little nearer the sea and copper mined in the hinterland was exported from its harbour. At the end of the 19th century, archaeologists uncovered a number of tombs from Marion's golden age; however, these have been filled in and are awaiting another round of excavations. Some of the finds from excavations have been gathered together at the excellent small **Marion/Arsinoë Archaeological Museum** (September to June Monday to Wednesday and Friday 8am–2pm, Thursday 9am–5pm; July to August Monday to Friday 8am–2pm, Saturday 9am–5pm; admission charge).The shingle beach, interspersed with sandy sections, extends for miles west, as far as the Baths of Aphrodite.

Only a few tracks and bridle paths cross the uninhabited ★ **Akamas peninsula**. This northeastern tip of Cyprus has survived as a habitat for rare plants and strongly-flavoured wild herbs such as sage and thyme. Environmental campaigners are to be thanked for saving the peninsula from tourist development (so far). As yet, the government's promise to declare the region a national park has not been honoured, and four-wheel-drives and motorbikes are driven through the woodland.

Peaceful Akamas

A road leads from Polis to the fishing and holiday village of **Lakki**. Formerly restricted to a thin strip of seafood restaurants and shops alongside a small fishing harbour, Lakki has spread inland in recent years and the harbour has been extended to accommodate a marina. This is the gateway to the Akamas, and many visitors choose to access the peninsula the easy way: by way of glass-bottom and 'barbecue' tour boats. A spring that once existed here was said to cause anyone who drank from it to fall head over heels in love with the first person they saw. Continue on foot and before long the path reaches ★ **Loutra tis Afroditis** (Baths of Aphrodite), hidden away in a fertile grove. According to legend, the goddess and her lover Adonis sought privacy here. Refreshingly cool water trickles from a rocky ledge into three natural basins. Bathing in the pool is said to bring beauty and eternal youth – not that you're allowed to enter to find out! Two ★ **nature trails** follow Aphrodite's footsteps further into the peninsula's interior. The couple are said to have rested at **Pyrgos tis Rigaenis**, a ruined monastery in the shade of some primeval oaks. Another tale links the place with Queen Regina and Digenis the Giant *(see page 77)*.

The villages near **Drouseia** in the **Laona** region are trying, with the support of money from the European Union, to create a 'gentler form of tourism'. The village school by the church square in Kathikas has been converted into a cultural centre, where slides provide information on the everyday life of the local farmers, on fauna and flora and possible walks. The road from Drouseia to **Neo Chorio**, via the abandoned Turkish village of **Androlikou**, is little used by traffic and so features in many walking tours.

Loutra tis Afroditis

The pilgrims' church of **Agios Georgios** at **Cape Drepano** overlooks a fishing harbour and a tiny beach. The foundations and mosaics of a basilica provide evidence that in late antiquity an important town once stood on the plateau, but little is known of its fate. The inhabitants buried their dead in rock tombs near the steps to the quay. Archaeologists hope that excavation work underway on the tiny offshore island of Geronisos will reveal more about the mysterious town, probably Ptolemaic in origin.

Exterior and interior of Agios Georgios

The once quiet hamlet of Cape Drepano – not much more than three *tavernas* – is gradually being hemmed in by villas owned mostly by expatriates, and the surrounding orchards are vanishing. It comes alive on Saturdays. Baptisms take place in the church and that is always an excuse for Cypriots to organise a lavish feast. Presents, votive offerings and wax figures of babies can be bought at the **market**. The faithful then offer them to the church saint. Single people still in search of a partner may find that visiting the **Byzantine church** will help to bring them love. Lighting a candle in the church might do the trick: say the name of the loved one three times and then turn the candle upside down. If it continues to burn, love and happiness will follow.

To the north of Agios Georgios, at **Lara Bay**, a coastal path runs beside a protected beach which serves as a breeding ground for two threatened species: the green turtle and the loggerhead turtle. The Cypriot authorities are working with the Worldwide Fund for Nature on the Lara Project, which aims to protect spawning females and newly hatched young turtles from both natural enemies and unthinking bathers. To avoid crushing any of the buried eggs, under no circumstance should you drive cars by the water's edge between June and August. One of the finest hikes in western Cyprus runs through the ★★ **Avakas Gorge**. Only at midday does the sun penetrate to the floor of this steep and narrow ravine. In places the path is in a stream fed by rock springs, but there is no cause for alarm: the water is not only shallow, but cool and refreshing. The path ends in a hollow with sides so steep that even goats find it difficult to negotiate. Anyone planning a day's walk to Arodes would be well advised to join a guided walking party.

Taking life easy

Coral Bay, a booming holiday village, marks the return to 'civilisation'. The resort is based around a fine beach that gets overwhelmed in high season both by local holidaymakers and by sand-starved sunbathers from Pafos. Just outside the resort is **Snake George's Reptile Park** (daily 10am–dusk; admission charge), where an Austrian enthusiast tries to spread a little tolerance for the island's diminishing snake population. Coral Bay is overlooked by Pegeia, a hill village that remains handsome despite the loss of virtually all of the farmland between it and the sea to an explosion of identikit villas. Corallia Bay, on the other side of the **Maa peninsula** (where there was a Bronze Age settlement), is popular with windsurfers.

Route 11

★★★ **Troodos** *See map on page 41*

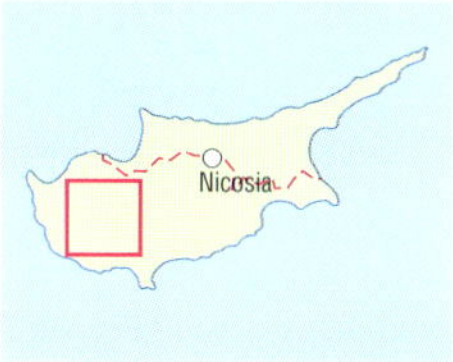

Pafos – Kykkos – Stavros tis Psokas forest station (130km/80 miles)

Thanks to a re-afforestation programme begun during the period of British colonial rule, Cyprus is the most densely wooded island in the Mediterranean. In the woods around Mount Olympos (1,953m/6,405ft), the island's highest mountain, there is a wide range of nature trails from which to choose. Perhaps the most beautiful of these paths winds for two hours through the various vegetation zones of the mountain, at the same time providing an insight into the geology of the region. It runs from the Troodos forest station along a mountain stream to the idyllic Kaledonian Falls and then on to Platres – a pleasant spot except at the height of summer. Forest tracks through deserted terrain lead to Kykkos, the richest monastery in Cyprus and close to where Archbishop Makarios is buried. Then it is on to the forest station at Stavros tis Psokas. To cover this route in a car, even without any long walks and the detour to Stavros tis Psokas, allow for a long day.

The wine village of ★ **Omodos** is certainly one of the prettiest places in Cyprus. The white houses with blue doors, shady vine arbours and lovingly tended flowers are reminiscent of the Cyclades Islands. Old women sit knitting in the shade of mulberry trees while sleepy cats sprawl on window ledges, the sales-orientated local tourist trade notwithstanding.

Amateur geologists should enjoy the two-hour walk from Omodos to Kato Platres. The vineyards end above

Shady Omodos

The Troodos foothills

Lunch break

the village where the valley narrows. It is not the climate nor the altitude that limits vine cultivation, but the soil. The light chalk on which vines thrive gives way abruptly to brownish-grey volcanic tuff. Around Kato Platres this changes to volcanic diabase before the primary rocks of the Troodos mountains push their way to the surface.

Because of its pleasantly cool summer climate, **Pano Platres** (1,128/3,699ft) has been a favourite with the British since colonial times. The predominant colours in Platres, a village hidden away amid dense woodland, are green and red. Brooks babble at the verges of steep roads and, out of season, a peaceful, almost weary atmosphere prevails. The principal occupation of the holidaymakers seems to be watching passers-by; and at the busiest times of the year, trying to thread their cars through the jams on the steep, narrow streets.

Trooditissa monastery (1,424m/4,670ft; closed to non-Orthodox visitors) is hidden away at the head of a fertile valley, under huge walnut and plane trees. Founded over a thousand years ago after an icon of Mary attributed to the evangelist Luke was discovered here, it became the summer residence of the Bishop of Pafos. But it has burnt down on more than one occasion since and the buildings are relatively recent. In the monastery church (1731), young women pilgrims come not only to worship the miracle-working Virgin Mary but also to put on a silver-coated belt which is said to help them to conceive a boy. The monastery is not open for casual visits.

A small holiday resort grew up at the village of **Troodos** (1,650m/ 5,412ft) during the British colonial era. *Tavernas*, hotels, stalls, a post office and a petrol station meet the needs of most visitors. Four relatively easy nature trails that can be followed wearing sports shoes start here. Leaflets about the walks should be available in boxes at the start and from the new **visitor centre** (tel: 25420144) in the resort. They show the route and give explanations in English about the sights. Most tourist offices also supply them.

The ★★ **Kaledonia Trail** follows a shady path down to Platres. It runs alongside a stream that flows even in summer and lower down tumbles noisily over a waterfall. Nature-lovers particularly will be interested in this trail with its changing range of vegetation. Troodos pines and rare black poplars thrive higher up; more typical for the medium altitudes are golden oaks, Aleppo pines and the bright reddish-brown strawberry trees that stand out through the thicket.The ★ **Artemis** or **Chionistra Trail** circles **Mount Olympos** (1,951m/6,401ft) without any steep gradients. Cypriots also call their highest mountain Chionistra, meaning 'frost-bite'. Two installations that mar the mountain's beauty are a radar station on the summit maintained by Britain's Royal Air Force and the Cyprus National Guard's command bunker. From December to the end of February the Cyprus Ski Club operates ski-lifts on the slopes.

In the spring, Marathassa valley is covered not with snow but with a veil of white cherry blossom. Quince, plums and pears also grow on the terraces that were painstakingly carved out of the hillsides by earlier generations. Many of the gardens have grown wild, reverting to their natural state.

Take a nature trail

Mount Olympos

A modest spa has been established in **Kalopanagiotis** around a spring of sulphurous water. Pilgrims come to visit the monastery of ★ **Agios Ioannis Lampadistis** (March to November Tuesday to Sunday 8am–1pm and 2–7pm [until 6pm March to May]; December to February, Tuesday to Sunday 8am–1pm and 2–4pm; free but donation appreciated) and its church murals, a UNESCO World Heritage site. The 11th-century cruciform basilica is noted for its fine frescoes. The narthex and Roman Catholic chapel were added in the 15th century and the murals here betray clear Western influences. In the 18th century another church roofed with barrel vaulting was added and the silver-coated skull of the town's patron saint is kept here. Olive and grape presses are displayed in the east wing of the monastery.

Kykkos monastery, mosaic detail

★ **Kykkos**, Cyprus's richest and most powerful monastery, lies in a remote spot surrounded by pine forest at 1,140m (3,740ft). The abbey formerly owned estates as far away as the Black Sea coast and it is still the biggest landowner on Cyprus. When the Turks plundered the monastery in 1821, they are said to have made off with 16 camel-loads of gold and silver. More pilgrims visit Kykkos than any other monastery on the island. Many of the visitors come to express their thanks for a miracle attributed to Kykkos and give presents or declare that the monastery is to be a beneficiary of their will. They no doubt hope that when the Day of Judgement comes, such acts of generosity will count in their favour.

The most important holy object is the icon of the Virgin Mary painted by St Luke which was presented to the monastery by the Byzantine emperor Alexis Comnenos in 1100. He was giving thanks to Isaiah, the monk who founded the monastery and who miraculously cured his daughter of gout. A silver mounting specially made in 1795 masks the icon, thought to be too sacred to gaze upon. No one has set eyes on it since that date.

On **Throni tis Panagia** or Our Lady's Throne, a short drive uphill from the monastery, lies the grave of Archbishop Makarios. This senior religious dignitary and first president of Cyprus started his career as a novice in Kykkos and for all his life had a close affinity with its religious community. A wishing tree hung with rags stands near his grave, testifying to the fact that Cypriots accord him almost saint-like status.

Cedar Valley

A cross-country vehicle is all but essential for anyone venturing further into the woods beyond Kykkos. Some 50,000 of the last surviving Troodos cedars grow in ★ **Cedar Valley**. These fine trees, larger and more beautiful than their Lebanese counterparts, can live for over 600 years. The rare and timid moufflon *(ovis ammon orientalis cyprius)* also lives in the valley. Just as the species was on the point of extinction, successful attempts were made to breed it in captivity, and the national airline, Cyprus Airways, has adopted it as its emblem. Without binoculars, you may wait a long time for a glimpse of this sheep-like creature in the wild.

The forest station at the idyllically located village of **Stavros tis Psokas** further up Cedar Valley keeps a herd of about 60 moufflon in a reserve.

Moufflon

Route 12

★ Keryneia (Girne) – Cyprus's picture-book harbour

The old harbour and home with the catch

The idyllic harbour set against the steeply rising Pentadaktylos/Beşparmak (Five Finger) mountain range makes Keryneia into one of the most attractive resorts on the island. In the bay, shaped like a horseshoe and dominated on the eastern side by a sturdy castle, fishing boats rock gently alongside fashionable yachts whose owners, at least during the summer season, probably prefer this formerly sleepy but increasingly bustling little town to the packed-to-the-gunwales marinas of the Aegean. In days gone by, the warehouses around the harbour were used to store locally produced carob and olive oil. Most have by now been converted into hotels and holiday apartments, while behind lie the ordinary homes of the local people. The promenade belongs to pedestrians – no cars disturb the peaceful atmosphere of souvenir shops, café terraces and *tavernas*.

History

It is thought that Keryneia was first settled in the 10th century BC by Greek Achaeans, but little is known about the town until it came under the control of King Nicocreon of Salamis (312BC). Although a castle and walls were built in the 8th or 9th century, the town was attacked and

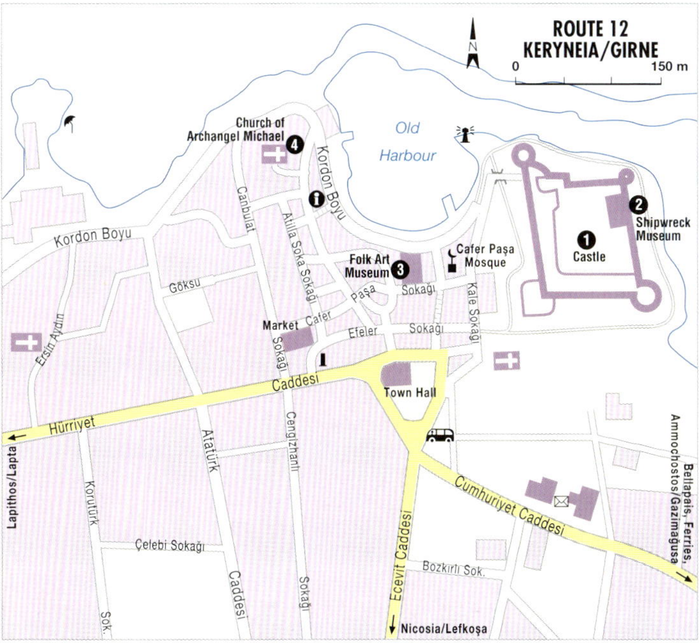

plundered by Arabs and pirates on a number of occasions. In 1192 the town and the family of the last Byzantine ruler fell into the hands of the Crusaders. Four centuries later, in 1570, the town and castle were captured by the Ottomans without a struggle. At the beginning of the 20th century many British officers, enticed by the mild climate, came to Keryneia either as tourists or to retire. For an idea of the atmosphere in northern Cyprus during the unsettled 1950s, read Lawrence Durrell's *Bitter Lemons*. The English writer lived for several years in nearby Belapaïs (Beylerbeyi).

Sights

Harbour fortress

The **castle** ❶ at Keryneia (daily 9am–7pm in summer; 9am–1pm and 2–4.45pm in winter; admission charge), built in the 8th century by the Byzantines, is the best-preserved harbour fortress on the island. The base of the round tower has survived from the earliest days and marks the northwest corner of the complex. At that time the Byzantine **Agios Georgios** chapel was located outside the castle. The Lusignans renovated the north and east and built the horseshoe-shaped **Northeast Tower** and also the living quarters in the inner courtyard – adding a touch of courtly elegance to military functionalism.

In the 16th century the Venetians modified the castle still further; they are responsible for its present design. In 1374 Genoese siege engines inflicted considerable damage to the walls and after the development of siege cannons, the fortress with its high, but rather weak walls, was too vulnerable to defend. Apart from the new **Northwest Tower**, there was no space for further reinforcement on the seaward side. But as a maritime power with galleys controlling the seas, the Venetian strategists mostly feared attacks from the land, so a new wall was constructed and the intervening land filled with earth and stones, thus creating a rampart 38m (125ft) thick. An impression of the strength of these fortifications can be gained from the long, slippery passageway which leads through them down into the casemates of the **Southwest Bastion**. The strengthened fort was never put to the test, though. In 1570 and without a shot being fired, the Venetian troops – demoralised by the fall of Nicosia – surrendered to the Ottoman admiral Sadık Paşa, who still guards over the entrance from his **sarcophagus** in the gatehouse.

Living from the sea

The **Shipwreck Museum** ❷ (daily 9am–7pm in summer; 9am–1pm and 2–4.45pm in winter; admission charge), on the east side of the castle courtyard, houses the hull of a sailing ship that sank or was scuppered by pirates some time between 288 and 262BC. At least four sailors went down with their ship and its cargo. Finds include the mariners' cutlery, amphoras filled with almonds and 26 mill stones, probably used as ballast.

The minaret of **Cafer Paşa Mosque** and two date palms tower above other roofs, making a picturesque sight when framed against the mountain backdrop. A small **Folk Art Museum** ❸ (Monday to Friday 9am–2pm in summer; 9am–1pm and 2–4.45pm in winter; admission charge) is accommodated in an old warehouse by the harbour and is well worth a visit. Completed in 1860, the dazzlingly white **church of the Archangel Michael** ❹ is, after the harbour and castle, the third symbol of Keryneia's past. A **collection of icons** (Monday to Friday 9am–2pm in summer; 9am–1pm and 2–4.45pm in winter; admission charge) awaits the visitor in what is, apart from the iconostasis, a plain interior. Sadly, these exhibits, collected from local churches, are poorly labelled.

As there are no beaches in Keryneia, to find one, follow the coast road to the east.

Excursions

For its position alone ★★ **Agios Ilarion** (daily 9am–4.30pm in summer; 9am–1pm and 2–4.45pm in winter; admission charge) must rank as one of the finest sights in northern Cyprus. This marvellous castle of battlements and towers seems to grow naturally out of the steep limestone rocks of the Pentadaktylos mountains.

Its name probably originates from a Palestinian monk who spent his twilight years in Cyprus (*c.*370), but the annals of sainthood contain 15 other pious men bearing the same name. A monastery emerged from the original settlement and then the Byzantines extended it into a castle in the 10th century. From 1228–32 Hilarion played a key role in Emperor Friedrich II's attempt to seize Cyprus, almost in passing, while on his way to the Holy Land during the 6th Crusade. Those loyal to the emperor and the supporters of the Lusignans exchanged the roles of besieger and besieged several times, until the emperor's army

Agios Ilarion

was eventually annihilated on the pass below the castle.

Agios Ilarion consists of three clearly defined wards, one above the other on the side of the hill. The stables and soldiers' quarters are at the lowest level; above them are the old monastery and refectory in which the Lusignans held their banquets. The climb to the upper ward of the badly decaying castle is hard work but, once there, the view over the coastal plain and out to sea will repay the effort. The best time to view the whole complex is early in the morning when the sun is in the right position for photographers.

In the rectory of Belapaïs

The Gothic ★★ **Belapaïs Abbey** ('Abbey of Peace'; daily 9am–7pm in summer; 9am–1pm and 2–4.45pm in winter; admission charge) stands in the heart of a sleepy village of the same name. Alongside the abbey stands the 'Tree of Idleness', made famous by Lawrence Durrell in his book *Bitter Lemons*. It is indeed a good place to take a rest. Augustinian monks founded a monastery here in 1205 and they were soon joined by monks from a Premonstrantensian order. The abbey's pointed arches and ribbed vaulting in northern French Gothic style ought to have looked out of place in this Levantine landscape but it seems to blend in well with the olive groves, cypresses and date palms. The Lusignan coat-of-arms above the entrance to the dining hall serves as a reminder of Belapaïs's royal benefactors: when Jerusalem fell, the Augustinians were expelled from the Holy Land and Hugo I donated extensive estates to the order. To the anger of the archbishop, Hugo III (1267–84) granted the abbot the right to wear a bishop's mitre during services. By the time the Ottomans arrived, Belapaïs was both structurally and morally disintegrating. A Venetian inspector who visited in the mid-15th century complained that the monks were not reading Mass, devoting themselves instead to their concubines and their children.

Belapaïs Abbey cloisters

Route 13

Forgotten sights by Morfou (Güzelyurt) Bay

Keryneia (Girne) – Soloi – Vouni (85km/53 miles)

A hire car is essential for this day trip *(see page 93)*. The itinerary starts by following the beaches along the north coast and then on to the citrus groves around the little country town of Güzelyurt (Turkish for 'beautiful country', Morfou in Greek). In the spring when the orange and citrus trees are in blossom, a delightful aroma spreads over the fertile plain. Below Soloi, a town that grew rich from copper deposits, the ore-processing and loading equipment quietly rusts away to create a modern industrial ruin. Archaeologists continue to ponder over who built Vouni Palace on the table mountain above the coast. Certainly none of the ancient writers mention it.

The town of **Karaman (Karmi)** was discovered initially by the British and many have second homes or have retired here. As many of the property owners stay for only a few weeks each year, their houses are often let as holiday homes. Ask locally for more information. Perhaps it was the presence of so many outsiders in the village that saved the outwardly rather unassuming church from damage during the Turkish invasion. The icons and iconostasis can usually be viewed late on Sunday mornings, but at the time of writing the church was closed for an undetermined period.

Thanks to the plentiful water supply from local springs, the region around **Lapithos (Lapta)** has enjoyed the benefits of fertile soil, a factor which attracted settlers as long ago as the Late Stone Age. The ancient city-state of Lapithos was situated near Karavas (Alsancak) beach, where the Turks landed on 20 July 1974. A concrete memorial marks the spot. Over a hundred years ago (on land now belonging to the military and not open to the public) near Acheiropoiitos monastery, farmers discovered a fine set of early Christian silver tableware. Some pieces from the buried treasure which had been hidden by the Arabs are displayed in the Cyprus Museum in Nicosia *(see page 20)*.

Morfou – famous for its fruit

Morfou (pop. 12,000) is situated in the middle of a huge citrus plantation. The fruit is packed or processed in the town's factories and sent for export. Until 1974 Morfou was largely Greek Cypriot; many of the present residents originated from the former Turkish wine-producing villages in the Troodos. The 18th-century monastery church of ★ **Agios Mamas** includes fragments from ancient structures. Under a Gothic arch, where panels recount the life story of the saint, lies the tomb of Agios Mamas. The

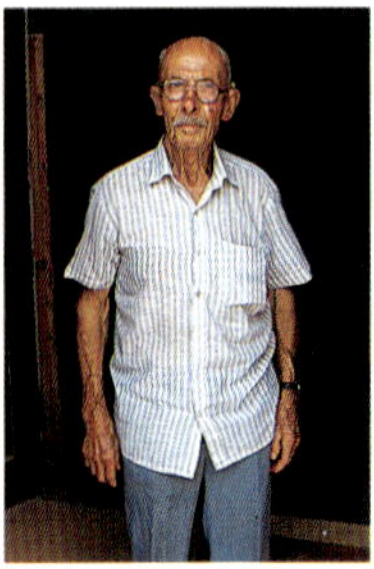

A local veteran

iconostasis with its painstakingly carved leafwork and the fighting mythical beast is a testimony to the craftsmanship of the Venetian period. Mamas can be seen on many of the icons and also as a relief on the west portal – where he is shown as a combination of shepherd and hermit – riding a lion with a lamb on his arm.

As well as a protector of animals, Mamas is revered as the patron saint of tax dodgers. According to folklore, one day Mamas was summoned to Nicosia to appear before the governor to explain why he had not paid any taxes. On the way, Mamas tamed a lion which was on the point of killing a lamb and rode off to the capital on its back. When the governor of Nicosia heard the news, he cancelled the meeting and it is said that the tax collectors never troubled Mamas again.

The key to the church is kept, as it always has been, in the episcopal palace, although now it is a natural history and archaeological museum (daily 9am–7pm in summer; 9am–1pm and 2–4.45pm in winter; admission charge). Its most famous exhibit is a statue of the multi-breasted goddess of fertility, Artemis of Ephesus, found in Salamis in 1980. A pair of golden earrings and some quaint terracotta lamps from the Hellenistic era are on display in the same room.

Solitary Soloi: the theatre

Karavostasi (Gemikonaği), or the 'ships' resting place', is now a truly restful place but it has not always been so. Abandoned slag heaps, rusting silos and a conveyor belt projecting out to sea bear witness to the fact that the town's harbour was once used for exporting copper ore. Mining started in antiquity and continued until the 1960s.

The ancient city of ★★ **Soloi** was founded in 600BC, when King Philokypros summoned the famous Athenian statesman and poet Solon to Cyprus and named the new city after him. As a result of its copper-mining industry, the city-state quickly flourished, but it was sacked

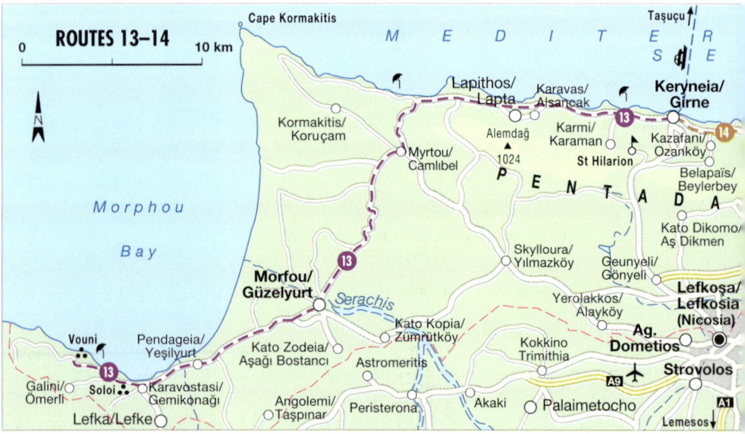

by the Persians in 498BC and ravaged by the Arabs in the 7th century AD. The British completed the job by carrying off much of the stone to help build the Suez Canal.

Soloi is noted for the 'Aphrodite of Soloi', unearthed by Swedish archaeologists over 60 years ago. This highly stylised statue has been used by the marketing department of the tourist board as a symbol for ancient Cyprus. Although the 2nd-century BC artefact occupies a place of honour in Nicosia's Cyprus Museum *(see page 20)*, it is now recognised to have been mass-produced by an unknown workshop. The rebuilt **Roman theatre** is worth seeking out. Not only does the auditorium have superb acoustics, but the seats offer a fine view out over the meadows and gardens as far as the horizon, where sea and sky merge in a haze. Mosaics on the floor of the **basilica** portray animals, including a fine swan. An inscription pleads, 'O Christ, save the person who donated this mosaic' but perhaps someone should plead for the mosaic as it is completely unprotected, facing exposure both to the elements and the footsteps of irresponsible visitors. Perhaps it is a blessing that only a fraction of the old town has been uncovered. The Canadian team working on the site had to end their project in 1974 for political reasons.

Floor mosaic in the basilica

On the road to Vouni

Between 498 and 449BC the ★ **Vouni Palace** (daily 9am–7pm in summer; 9am–1pm and 2–4.45pm in winter; admission charge), on a hill 235m (770ft) above sea level, was the residence of the Persian governor, who no longer felt safe in Soloi and considered the inhabitants hostile. The bathing complex, consisting of steam bath, caldarium and frigidarium, was technically on a par with the baths the Romans built centuries later. Only the palace foundations remain following a fire in the 4th century; however the atmosphere and view make a visit worthwhile.

Vouni Palace

Route 14

From coast to coast *See map on pages 64–5*

Keryneia (Girne) – Pentadaktylos mountains – Famagusta (Ammochostos/Gazimağusa) (160km/100 miles)

Pentadaktylos mountain

Like the pointed crest of a dragon, the Five Finger mountains (Greek name: Pentadaktylos; Turkish: Beşparmak) extend from Cape Kormakitis (Korucam) along the north coast and across the island as far as the Karpasia (Kirpaşa) peninsula. Where the rocks are at their steepest, Voufaventon (Buffavento) castle clings to a rugged mountain top almost 1,000m (3,250ft) above sea level. The abandoned Antifonitis and Sourp Magar monasteries lie hidden away in the woods, and the wide range of Cyprus's flora is catalogued in the herbarium at the Halevka (Alevkaya) forest station. The Mesaoria (Mesarya) plain on the southern flank of the mountain range contains little of interest. Anyone coming from Keryneia and not wishing to go on to Famagusta can miss out the second half of this route. To complete this route in a day, a car is essential, although the little-used forest tracks in the mountains are ideal for walkers and mountain bikers.

Pottery for sale

Start out on the new coast road from Keryneia, passing the Acapulco, Lara and Alagadi beaches. A kilometre (⅔ mile) before the junction to Charkeia (Karaağac), explorers with a good sense of direction (look for the remnants of the old coast road and follow the fragments of pottery) can investigate the ruins of the old port of **Charkeia** which lies between the road and the sea. What looks at first sight to be an idyllic bay turns out on closer inspection to be awash with plastic debris and other rubbish. The prevailing currents mean that refuse tipped into the Mediterranean in the Middle East and from passing ships sweeps round to Turkey and then south to the beaches of Cyprus.

Above **Agios Amvrosios (Esentepe)** in a dense mixed forest lies the monastery of ★ **Antifonitis**, or the 'echo' monastery, so-called because of its position in a hollow. The last 500m (1,600ft) of the steep descent are best covered on foot. A superb *liquiambar styraciflua* tree, whose resin was used by the monks to make incense, marks the entrance to the monastery. It stands in a clearing, which in early spring is carpeted with red poppies.

Antifonitis is Cyprus's last Byzantine monastery (12th-century) where the dome does not rest on four but on eight supports. While it is true that the chapel on Mount Hilarion is of the eight-pillar type, the dome there has collapsed. Many frescoes have been destroyed, often as a result of art thieves. The Archangel Michael, for example, in the late Comnenian apse was badly damaged when someone tried to remove it. More skilful thieves set their sights on Gabriel. Where his face once was, a gaping hole remains. In some places wall paintings have been removed by specialists and faded but older pictures of the saints have come to light.

During the holiday period, **Halevka (Alevkaya)**, in the heart of lush pine forests and refreshingly cool in the summer, is a popular place for Turkish Cypriots to indulge in their favourite hobby, the barbecue. There is also a restaurant open at weekends. One room in the forestry centre houses an unexpected attraction, a herbarium. The British botanist Deryck Viney has painstakingly catalogued practically all 1,200 of northern Cyprus's plant species. Many of them have been dried, pressed and illustrated. Plant-lovers will be enthralled by photographs of rare orchids, clearly demonstrating the wealth of exotic flora that exists on the island. The plants that have been preserved in formalin may interest the expert, but they bear no comparison with the splendour of the living plant.

The barbecue is a popular pastime

The Armenian **Sourp Magar** monastery was targeted during the Turkish invasion and destroyed. Even if it was of little interest from an art historian's point of view, it is sad that the seeds of the hatred between Turks and Armenians, that has lasted for almost a century, have here, on neutral soil, yielded such a bitter fruit.

Just before the mountain track joins the metalled road, the striking ★ **Pentadaktylos (Five Finger)** mountain (740m/2,427ft), that has given its name to a whole mountain range, presents an inviting challenge to the energetic. With stout shoes and a little experience of hill-walking, it is possible to reach the deepest notch in the ridge and enjoy a windy view as far as the coast; however, an ascent of the steep limestone rock at the summit should be attempted only by fully equipped climbers.

Voufaventon

★★ **Voufaventon (Buffavento)**, 954m/3,129ft, or 'where the wind blows', is Cyprus's castle of superlatives: it is the highest, the hardest to reach, has suffered the greatest destruction over the centuries and is the least well researched. It is a marvel how the Byzantines levelled out the terrain of pointed rocks and steep slopes to create a flat surface on which to build. At least walls or expensive fortifications were not required, given the dizzying height and the near-vertical drop beneath it. The sombre fortress, often shrouded in mist, was used as a prison during the Middle Ages. A royal courtier, Jean de Visconte, was incarcerated here after an amorous adventure with a Lusignan queen. He was chained up and left without food for weeks before his death.

Famagusta ruins

Smoking a hookah

Route 15

★ Famagusta (Ammochostos/Gazimağusa)– city of fallen splendour *See maps on pages 69 and 72.*

With the partition of Cyprus, Famagusta became a sleeping beauty. In the old town, protected by massive ramparts, Gothic church ruins reach skyward and Byzantine chapels lie hidden among gardens and vegetable fields. For a long time now, the inhabitants of the town, known to the Turkish Cypriots as Mağusa or Gazimağusa and to the Greek Cypriots as Ammochostos, have had room to spare within their walled enclosure. There were said to be 365 churches, almost certainly a symbolic and exaggerated number, but a good two dozen abandoned churches can still be found. Very few concrete buildings mar the old town.

Barbed wire is strewn across the beach, blocking off the hotel quarter of Varosha (Maraş), until 1974 Cyprus's most important tourist area. It is now accessible only to UN troops and the Turkish military. Holidaymakers make for the wide sandy beaches north of the town, and of course they are still allowed to visit the old town.

History

Ptolemy II founded the city in the 3rd century BC and named it after his wife Arsinoë. Only after the destruction of neighbouring Salamis by the Arabs in AD648 did Famagusta develop as a town. Its heyday was in the years following the eviction of the Crusaders from the Holy Land. After the fall of Acre in 1291, Famagusta, now on the eastern edge of the Christian sphere of influence, became an important meeting place for merchants from East and West. Christian refugees from Palestine settled here and the various Christian communities sought to outdo each other by building bigger and finer churches. Rich merchants concerned for the salvation of their souls endowed more places of worship. Western pilgrims, whose journals provide a picture of life in Famagusta, enthused over its cosmopolitan atmosphere.

In 1372 Famagusta fell into the hands of the Genoese, who squeezed it remorselessly, driving out the international traders with their customs duties and taxes. Even when the Venetians held sway here (1489–1571), the town never recaptured its former glory.

A victim of world politics

When Ottoman troops under Lala Mustafa Paşa landed on Cyprus in March 1570, Famagusta's fate was already sealed. Although there was an outcry throughout the Christian world and a fleet was despatched to assist fellow Christians in distress, the level of support was inadequate. The Spanish admiral had received secret orders from Philip II that the venture should not succeed as the Spaniards had no interest in helping their Venetian rivals. So, while the Ottomans tightened the siege on Famagusta, the galleys of the allied forces had already stopped rowing towards Cyprus. On 1 August 1571 the defending forces were starved into submission.

The Venetian lion

Sights

The principal attractions in the old town, apart from the churches, are the imposing fortifications, built to plans by

Giovanni Sanmicheli (d. 1558), a nephew of the celebrated military engineer Michele Sanmicheli. If time permits, a tour of the 3-km (2-mile) walls, with their 15 bastions, is very worthwhile.

The old fortifications

Entry to the old town is via the **Land Gate** ❶, first opened by the Ottomans. Before then, access was gained by a drawbridge and through **Ak Kule** ❷ (White Castle).

Istiklâl Caddesi, one of the town's busiest shopping streets, leads to the **Palazzo del Proveditore** ❸, the palace of the Venetian governor. The Turkish poet and journalist Namik Kemal (1840–88) was held prisoner in one of the wings. At the time a rebellious free-thinker, he is now revered as a pioneer of the modern Turkish state.

His bust can be seen in the main square in the shade of a huge sycamore. It is said to be 700 years old and must be the oldest tree on the island. It even predates the construction (1298–1326) of the Roman Catholic cathedral of ★ **St Nicholas** ❹, now known as the **Lala Mustafa** mosque or in local parlance the **Agia Sofia** mosque. After the cathedral of St Sophia in Nicosia, St Nicholas was the second coronation church of the Lusignans. Following the formal abdication of Caterina Cornaro, the last queen of Cyprus, Lusignan rule of Cyprus ended here. With its west front, based on Rheims cathedral, and the fine tracery above the side doors, it is regarded as a masterpiece of Gothic architecture. An earthquake and cannon fire from the Ottoman besiegers damaged the towers. The minaret was added by Muslims.

Cathedral of St Nicholas

The seaward side of the **sea gate** ❺ (1496) boasts a fine lion of St Mark and the city side is also guarded by a stone lion. According to legend, treasure was hidden in his gullet. If it was ever discovered, the finder has kept quiet about it.

Above the main entrance to the **citadel**, the **Othello Tower** ❻ (daily 9am–7pm in summer; 9am–1pm and 2–4.45pm in winter; admission charge) is carved with the name of the architect Foscarini alongside another lion of St Mark. The tower bears the name of Shakespeare's tragedy because the tale of the Moor of Venice, Desdemona and Iago was set in Cyprus and historians have suggested that a Venetian governor of Famagusta by the name of Christopher Moro was the Moor.

Another no less bloody tale surrounds the **Canbulat Bastion** ❼ (daily 9am–7pm in summer; 9am–1pm and 2–4.45pm in winter; admission charge), easily recognisable as a lighthouse. At the time of the Turkish siege, the Venetians protected it with a device made of rotating knives that threatened to cut any intruder to pieces. The brave Canbulat threw himself and his horse at the device, destroyed it and thus enabled the Turkish attackers to advance. His grave forms the centrepiece of a small **museum** where the exhibits document the history of the town. Outside the entrance lie memorial tombs to the victims of the civil war. Photographers will appreciate the view over the old town.

The district of **Varosha** with its fine beach and more than 80 hotels was once the jewel in Cyprus's tourist industry but since 1974 it has been a ghost town. It borders the demarcation line and is now controlled by Turkish forces. Fearing a protracted and bloody battle over the properties in this largely Greek Cypriot quarter, the invading army did not originally impose an occupying force. They only entered once it was clear that the residents had all fled in panic. As a bargaining counter in negotiations, Varosha is closed even to Turkish Cypriots.

Only the northernmost tip of Varosha beach near the Palm Beach Hotel is accessible. Other good beaches can be found by the ruins of Salamis and the hotels nearby.

Canbulat museum: tomb inscription

Excursions

Visitors to the excavations of **Egkomi** near the village of Tuzla will need a good imagination or else training as archaeologists. The foundations of Cyprus's first important town and an important centre of the copper industry dating from 2000BC are nothing more than a jumble of stone walls. Even what is thought to be the grave of **Niccreon**, the last king of Salamis, who preferred to cast himself into the flames of his burning palace than to give himself up to Ptolemy, is from a layman's point of view simply a mound of earth at the western exit of Tuzla.

Of more interest is the monastery of **St Barnabas**. Outsize paintings on the walls of the monastery church (1756) recount the story of the founding of the Cypriot Orthodox church. In 478, guided by a vision, Archbishop Anthemios discovered the grave of Barnabas. As the church could therefore be traced back to an apostle, it was entitled

Icon in St Barnabas's

Weavers at work in the monastery

The skeleton of a horse

Salamis

to demand independence *(autokephalia)* from the other Orthodox patriarchs. An **archaeological museum** (daily 9am–7pm in summer; 9am–1pm and 2–4.45pm in winter; admission charge) in the former monastery displays a selection of finds made after 1974, including some superb terracotta votive offerings.

The road to Salamis passes close to the **royal necropolis** where rulers and nobles were buried between the 8th and 6th centuries BC. Although all the 150 known graves were plundered both in antiquity and during the Middle Ages, a number of burial offerings have survived. Jewellery, clay vessels and furniture are displayed in Nicosia's Cyprus Museum *(see page 20)*. Horses drew the funeral bier to the tomb, were killed and then buried alongside their royal masters. Their skeletons have been preserved and can be seen under glass. Early Christians covered the **Prison of St Catherine** (tomb no. 50) with barrel vaulting. The princess who converted to Christianity is said to have been incarcerated here by her family. The chapel has been on the itinerary of pilgrims to the Holy Land since the late Middle Ages.

According to legend, ★★ **Salamis** (daily 9am–7pm in summer; 9am–1pm and 2–4.45pm in winter; admission charge) was founded by Teukros, a Trojan warrior mentioned

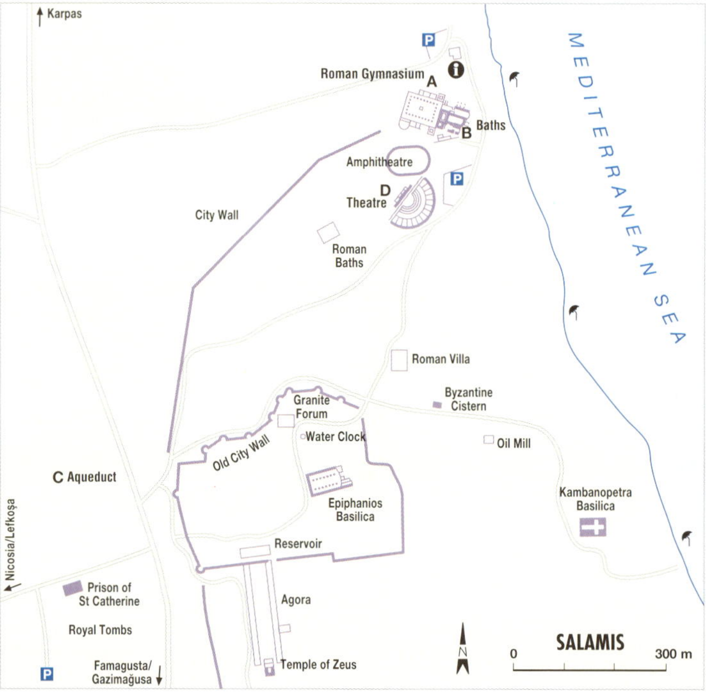

in Homer's *Iliad*. He named the city after his birthplace, an island south of Athens. In the 10th century BC Salamis took over from the abandoned Egkomi as an important trading centre. At its peak as many as 120,000 people lived in Cyprus's biggest town, but under the Romans it ceded its leading role to Pafos. In the 7th century AD, Salamis was finally abandoned and the inhabitants moved to Famagusta. It had been badly hit by an earthquake, had suffered a number of attacks by Arabs and the harbour had silted up.

Only a fraction of the town has been excavated. With the exception of one older tomb, the buildings date from the Hellenistic and Roman eras. Allow plenty of time for a full visit. Although Cyprus's largest open-air museum covers a wide area, it is worth trying to see as much as possible. Try to end up at the beach near the ruined site where acacias, eucalyptus trees and pines provide ample shade for a picnic. In spring the blossom is stunning. Visitors in a hurry will probably have to restrict their tour to the following highlights.

A good head shorter

The **Roman gymnasium [A]** was built above an older Hellenistic wrestling school but, with its courtyard surrounded by a shaded colonnade, it was more than just a centre for sporting activities. The menfolk would meet here to discuss politics and philosophy and to conduct their business rather as in a modern coffee house. However, as with all public buildings, only an elite sector of the community, i.e. those with Roman citizenship, were allowed access. The statues, the finest of which are on display in Nicosia's Cyprus Museum *(see page 20)*, were all beheaded. The culprits were probably early Christians who saw the statues as symbols of paganism, but Venetian souvenir hunters are also suspected.

Directly adjacent to the eastern colonnade are the **baths [B]**. The remains of mosaics showing scenes from Greek mythology can be seen in the niches of the sudatorium (sweating room) to the southeast. With the advent of Christianity or at the latest during the iconoclastic period, the niches were bricked up to conceal the pagan pictures from the eyes of guests. Water for the baths and the rest of the town arrived via an **aqueduct [C]**, traces of which are still visible at the junction with the road to the royal necropolis. Kythrea, about 60km (37 miles) away, was the source of the town's water.

The Roman theatre and local guides

To reach the Roman **theatre [D]** pass the stadium and the remains of an arena. With space for between 15,000 and 20,000 spectators, the theatre was one of the biggest in the Mediterranean. In antiquity a Dionysos altar would have stood in the middle of the semi-circular orchestra. Twenty of the 50 rows have been restored and, during the summer, plays and folk-music performances are occasionally put on here.

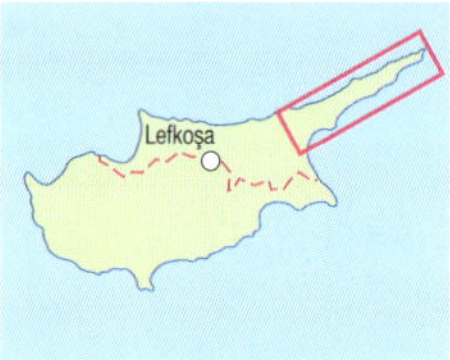

Route 16

The Karpasia (Kirpaşa) peninsula

Famagusta – Monastery of Agios Andreas (130km/ 80 miles)

Isolated beach on the peninsula

The isolated beaches of the Karpasia peninsula form one of the last coastal areas where turtles can still lay their eggs without being disturbed. On early summer nights – as long as they are not disturbed by light or noise – the 250kg (550lb) females crawl ashore, dig out a hole in the sand and lay about 40 tennis-ball-sized eggs. Provided the eggs are not discovered by foxes, unearthed by children building sandcastles or destroyed by car tyres, after about two months the baby turtles will emerge from their eggs, push their way out of the sand and hurry towards the water. (Cars should be kept off the sand from June onwards to avoid harming the turtle eggs.)

On the route itself, ruined churches and mosaics testify to a lively past. In one or two villages that the road passes through, an ageing minority, no more than a few hundred Greeks, refused to join the exodus to the south in 1974 and stayed put; most of the inhabitants, however, are now Turks from the mainland.

Tourers who have hired a car for the trip in Famagusta should plan for at least one overnight stop in Rizokarpaso (Dipkarpaz), or at one of the coast hotels.

Freshly caught fish

In **Trikomo (Iskele)** the cruciform **Panagia Theotokos** basilica has been converted into an icon museum (Monday to Friday 9am–2pm in summer; 9am–1pm and 2–4.45pm in winter; admission charge). Of most interest are the 12th-century, courtly-style frescoes, showing scenes from the Resurrection of Christ, which can be admired in the south dome and by the arch in front of the apse.

It is hard to resist the sandy beach lined with sunbeds and parasols near the quay in the fishing village of **Bogazi**

(**Boğaz**). The restaurants here specialise in serving freshly caught fish and it might be worth making a note of one or two for the return journey.

★ **Kantara castle** is a half-hour walk from Kantara village, another summer resort. This imposing fortification, the furthest east of the three castles on the **Pentadaktylos (Beşparmak)** ridge, was built in the 10th century to defend the surrounding countryside from repeated Arab attacks. Later, during the 14th and 15th centuries, the castle helped the Lusignans keep in check their Genoese adversaries who had established themselves in Famagusta. The Venetians eventually abandoned not only Kantara, but also St Hilarion and Buffavento. Maintaining mountainside castles was not a high priority for a naval power.

Kantara castle

On the edge of **Agias Trias (Sipahi)** are the remains of the 5th-century **Agia Trias** basilica. Apart from a few column stumps, some mosaics with imaginative geometric designs, similar to the type which are widespread in Syria, have survived.

In **Rizokarpaso**, the biggest town on the peninsula, the 'White Church' of **Agios Synesios** stands in the shadow of a new mosque. A few Greek Cypriots have remained here and retain their own coffee house and a small primary school.

The cruciform basilica of **Agios Philon** was built in the 10th or 11th century from the ruins of **Karpasia**, a town sacked by the Arabs, and now gives its name to the peninsula. Photographers will appreciate the sight of the church set against the blue of the sea and the green of a few palm trees. The track ends in **Afentrika (Effendiler)**. Thistles and scrub cover a ruined site (possibly Urania) that awaits excavation. A small church, clearly of Lusignan origins, is still in reasonable condition.

Monastery of the Apostle Andrew

A metalled road follows the south side of the peninsula to the ★ monastery of the **Apostle Andrew**. It was here that the brother of St Peter is said to have come ashore. Apparently, his thirsty crew dug out a rock to find a spring whose water still flows in a Frankish chapel.

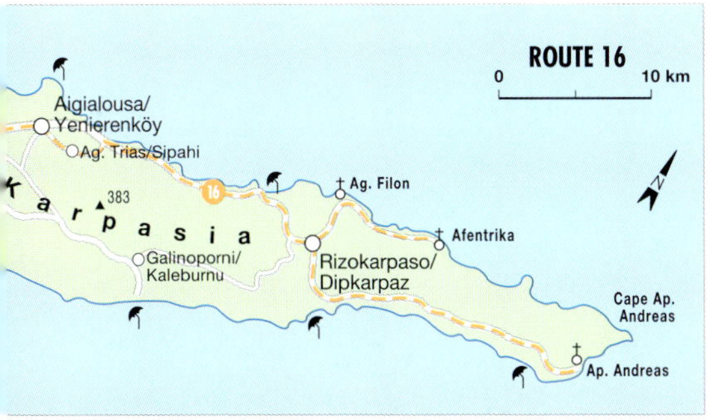

Legendary Figures

Opposite: Aphrodite

Aphrodite, born of the sea foam

Hesiod knew how to tell a good story: in his *Theogony* he recounted how Uranus the god of the sky hated the children that his wife Gaia the earth goddess produced and he thrust the young Titans back into their mother's womb. But Gaia was capable of defending herself. She made a sickle with sharp teeth and gave it to Kronos, her bravest son. One night when the lustful Uranus visited Gaia, Kronos was waiting for him and castrated him. The Erinyes (the Furies: goddesses of vengeance) and the Gigantes (giants) were born from the blood shed by Uranus. Kronos cast Uranus's severed organs into the sea. White foam *(aphros)* appeared and this turned into a girl: Aphrodite, born of foam. She swam to Kythera, but finding little to please her on the barren island turned to Cyprus. Eros and Himeros, the god of love's double, became Aphrodite's inseparable companions.

Aphrodite is a goddess with more facets to her character than simply passion. She was worshipped as a goddess of war until the patriarchal ancient Greeks stripped her of her weapons. She was also worshipped in Cyprus as Aphroditos, a bearded man.

The giant and the queen

Digenis (also known as Romios) is a giant of amazing strength often used by adults to threaten disobedient Cypriot children. He is a good-natured giant, but not blessed with intelligence. In many stories he fights against the Saracens, driving them off with boulders or else delivering a fatal blow. Once, when Digenis stumbled to the ground, the imprint of his little finger created Pentadaktylos (Five Finger mountain). It is there where the clever and cunning Queen Regina ('Rigena' in Greek) lives in grand chambers deep inside the mountain, beneath the abandoned Crusader castle. Sometimes the breathtakingly beautiful queen appears before the shepherds and distracts them, but woe betide anyone who tries to enter her treasure vault. In Regina, Aphrodite and the Near-Eastern mother goddesses live on but her halo comes from Mary, the mother of Jesus. She thus links ancient and modern religions.

Five Finger mountain

The countryside around Pafos once belonged to Regina and the Fabrica Hills were her palace. When the plain was afflicted by a terrible drought, she asked the giant Digenis to bring water from the mountains. He was happy to obey, hoping that by helping the beautiful queen he could win her hand. But the queen merely thanked the giant for his help and fled from his advances via an underground passage linking Fabrica with the Sanctuary of Aphrodite. Beside himself with anger, Digenis attacked her palace with a stone, the Digenis Rock *(see page 45)*.

Art History

Situated at the crossroads of three continents, Europe, Asia and Africa, Cypriot culture has been exposed to a wide variety of influences. And yet until the advent of Hellenism, Cypriot art managed to retain a unique character. While accepting outside influences, it expressed them in a typically Cypriot way.

Prehistory and antiquity

Before the Bronze Age, Cypriot civilisation displayed many insular features. Round huts and the occasional use of cornelian indicate links with the Syrian-Mesopotamian region, while the use of obsidian confirms that contacts existed with Anatolia.

One splendid example of prehistoric Cypriot art dates from the Early Bronze Age (2500–1900BC). The terracotta Shrine of Vouni is now displayed in the Cyprus Museum in Nicosia. The clay miniatures were designed for a mysterious ritual in which men wore bull masks and probably a child was sacrificed. The highlight of Cypriot terracotta art came in the Cypro-Archaic period (700–475BC) with the votive offerings of Agia Eirini (Akdeniz). Finds include bulls, chariots, warriors, priests and worshippers, a total of 2,000 strangely rigid figures, many oversized and similar to the clay figurines found in the tomb of China's first emperor in the city of Xian.

Female idols dating from the Copper Age and made from clay and steatite have been found. These are associated with the mother-worshipping sects that were widespread in the Near East. The later Aphrodite and Virgin Mary cults are continuations of the same theme.

With the discovery of copper, Cyprus came to occupy a much more important role in Mediterranean trade. Material prosperity created the conditions for artists to express themselves. Copper, bronze, ivory and gold were now available for their use.

During the Classical era, sculptures carved from limestone came into fashion. Although Cyprus was at first under the political control of the Persians, artists looked west to the Greek world. But with the start of the Hellenistic period (331–58BC) Alexandrian influences also played a part. One example is the famous Aphrodite of Soloi (2nd century BC). With Ptolemaic Egyptian domination during the years of Hellenism followed by the increasing influence of the Romans, Cypriot artistic expression reached new heights. In the realm of architecture, luxurious villas for the wealthy, baths and gymnasiums were built, all adorned with sophisticated mosaics. Those uncovered in Pafos and Kourion are excellent examples.

Greek head in Nicosia

Roman mosaic in Pafos

Early Christian art

During the years of rule from Byzantium, sacred images were systematically destroyed through the fervour generated by Iconoclasm (746–843), when religious fanatics strictly interpreted the Third Commandment (Thou shalt not make unto thee a graven image ...). Consequently, few early Christian mosaics have survived in the Eastern church. One remains at Kiti near Larnaka and another, the Mosaic of Lythragkomi (Boltağli), is on display in the Byzantine Museum and Art Galleries in Nicosia. This was illegally exported to the USA in 1974 but has been returned.

Many of the early Christian churches were destroyed by Arab invaders, but there are ruins, such as those at Kourion and Salamis, which are worth investigating.

Byzantine churches and Orthodox painting

Cyprus is a treasure trove of Byzantine art. There are few countries in the Orthodox Christian world where so many masterpieces of Byzantine art – from the 11th to the 18th century – can be found within such a small area. One architectural curiosity, which is only found in Cyprus, is the 'barn church' of which there are several examples in the Troodos mountains *(see pages 55–8)*. From the 13th century these cruciform churches in Byzantine style were covered with a weatherboard roof for extra protection against the winter snows.

The interiors of many Greek Orthodox churches are richly decorated with icons and frescoes, and those in Cyprus are no exception. To many Westerners the rigid and formal execution seems odd but, to understand icons in the

Byzantine 'barn church' and fresco

Interior of St John the Evangelist

Orthodox church, you need to examine their function. Unlike Western sacred art which aims to represent biblical scenes in a totally realistic way, Greek Orthodox art seeks to create a supernatural, mythical dimension in which the past, present and divine somehow merge with one another. In this way, the stories recounted in the Bible cease to be unique events and acquire a timeless character.

By idealising concepts of the eternal and the sublime, the saint on the icon becomes ever-present. Just how difficult it is to express spiritual concepts using worldly forms was demonstrated by the response of the iconoclasts, the Greek Orthodox fundamentalists who set out to destroy icons and religious images (AD726–843). These opponents of icons saw it as blasphemy to portray Christ and the apostles figuratively, but the icon painters solved the problem by establishing a set of commonly understood formulae and symbols which allowed little room for individual expression.

Pantocrator in the dome

The most important models, passed down through the generations, are the 'acheiropoeita', the pictures of Christ that were 'not painted by human hand'. These include the cloth that bore Christ's facial imprint. The icons which the evangelist Luke is said to have painted were also part of the repertoire because Luke saw Jesus and Mary face to face and was a witness to many of the events described in the New Testament.

Fresco painting also has its own set rules in the Orthodox Church, with Jesus the Pantocrator (Almighty) occupying pride of place in the dome, the prophets in the drum, the apostles in the pendentives, and so on. It is important to differentiate between the elegant, courtly style and the ascetic approach of the monks, both of which were subject to the increasing suppression of the Orthodox church by the Roman Catholic church via the Crusaders.

Sinan Paşa mosque, the former Church of Saints Peter and Paul

Western and Turkish influences

Grand Gothic churches were built under the Lusignans. The Venetians and the Genoese who followed built huge fortifications to protect the towns from invasion by the Turks. Mural painting continued to flourish in the Orthodox churches, and from about 1500, the influence of the Italian Renaissance becomes evident. But with the Ottoman conquest of Cyprus, practically every type of religious art ceased with the exception of icon painting. Churches were converted into mosques but none of the spaciousness of Seljuk and Ottoman architecture found its way on to the island. The Muslims simply added a minaret to the church, marked the direction of Mecca by a *mihrab* and removed all Christian imagery and decorations. Very few new mosques were built during the Turkish era, although caravanserais and fortifications were constructed.

Festivals

Carnival, has survived from the Venetian era. It begins on the 60th day before the Orthodox Easter festival. The 'foolish men and women' of Limassol go crazy.

Kataklysmos usually falls around Whitsuntide. It recalls the saving of Noah during the flood. In coastal towns, particularly Larnaka, the festival is celebrated with processions of boats, singing competitions and a fair *(see below)*.

Anthestiria. This flower festival on a Sunday in May in Pafos goes back to the ancient mysteries when the wine god Dionysos was honoured.

Limassol Festival. The most respected cultural festival on the island, held in July, started off as a folklore festival but in recent years it has included other art forms such as film, drama and an artists' fair. Performances are held in the inner courtyard of the castle.

Wine festival. For two weeks in September, throngs of people head for the municipal park in Limassol for free samples of the new wine.

Dressed for the occasion

Kataklysmos – the festival of the flood

Compared with the great Christian festivals of Easter, Christmas and the Feast of the Assumption (15 August), Whitsuntide plays only a minor role in the Cypriot Greek Orthodox calendar – except in Larnaka. For a whole week the town celebrates the *kataklysmos*. The seafront promenade disappears beneath rows of stands selling sweet delicacies such as *loukoumades* (honey puffs), *loukoumia* (don't call it Turkish delight) and *soujoukko* (almonds enclosed in a solidified grape-juice syrup). Teenagers show off their skills to their sweethearts in the shooting galleries. Musicians, poets, and dance troupes vie for attention.

The religious character of the festival becomes clear on Whit Monday. The priest blesses the sea and throws a cross into the water; then a scrum of young men dive in after it and try to fish it out. The *kataklysmos* is about the saving of Noah and the whole of humanity from the flood. Clearly, with the flood theme as the basis for the carnival, its roots go back a long way into the pre-Christian era. Many observers have noted how the biblical story resembles the Greek myth told about Deukalion (son of Prometheus) and his wife Pyrrha, who were the only survivors from the flood that Zeus used as a punishment for the crimes of Lycaon. Other researchers see a connection with Aphrodite's water rites. Whatever its origins, this boisterous and carefree festival is lots of fun.

MEZE HOME MADE 24 DISHES
PLEASE MAKE-A-RESERVATION
Beans Casserole 150
Dolmades Salad 200
Moussaka >> 200
Pot Roast 270
Liver onions (Lamb) 270
Lamb Chops Chips 250
STARTERS from 100
OMELETTES Chips from 130
SANDWICHES >> 80c
NES CAFE 50c
Greek Coffee 30
tea 40
Filter coffee 75
ALL TAXES ARE INCLUDED

Food and Drink

Opposite: Cypriot menu

The choice of food in Cyprus is extraordinarily wide, reflecting many different influences. Greek, Turkish and Lebanese dishes all feature on menus; even some British specialities are now firmly established in the Cypriot repertoire. To make the most of the local dishes, ask expressly for Cypriot fare, making it clear to the proprietor of the restaurant that you did not come to Cyprus to eat steak and chips; these taste better at home anyway.

Outdoor dining, Pafos

Cherries straight from the tree

With the exception of pork, which Muslims do not eat, before partition there was very little difference between a Turkish and a Greek menu. With the arrival of many thousands of Turks from the Anatolian mainland, however, the type of food available in Turkish shops and restaurants in the North changed to meet their requirements.

A rôtisserie grill, whether it is a small one with a battery-driven electric motor or the commercial variety where 30 spits are rotated at the same time, is an essential piece of household equipment. **Souvlakia** (Turkish *Şişkebap*), grilled chunks of meat, is the favourite grilled dish, closely followed by fish, which is usually cooked over charcoal. The grilling is done outside near the kitchen, behind the house, in the street, in the woods, anywhere. The barbecue picnic has become the Cypriots' favourite outdoor pastime, with the distinctive and appetising aroma of charcoal (or dried wood from olive and other trees) and sizzling meat a permanent feature of country life at weekends.

Mezedhes (Turkish *mezeler*), found on almost every menu, provide a good introduction to Cypriot cooking. In Greece and the Lebanon, these little nibbles are served as an hors d'oeuvre, but in Cyprus they make a complete meal and one for which the guest requires both plenty of time and a healthy appetite. For the price of a meal, as many as 20 small bowls are served in succession, some hot, some cold.

As well as the **estiatorion** (Turkish *restoran*) and the more popular **taverna** (Turkish *lokanta*), there is also the fish restaurant, the **psarotaverna** (Turkish *balïk lokantasi*). Food is served late into the night in the **kentro** or the **bouzoukitaverna**, with the added bonus of music and dancing. Deliciously sweet delicacies are available from the **zacharoplastion** (Turkish *pastahane*).

Drinks

In the Greek sector wine is an important export commodity. In a restaurant it is safe to choose the older vintages, but in a supermarket, where it is not so easy to return an oxidised bottle, it is better to opt for a more recent year. *Commandaria*, a Cypriot speciality, is a dessert wine, similar to port in both its method of production and its taste. A good *Commandaria* needs at least 10 years in the barrel before being bottled. The few wines from Turkish Cypriot vineyards have still some way to go before meeting modern standards and it is probably better to ask for a Turkish import.

A Greek coffee

Locally produced sherry or brandy sour, a long drink made from brandy, angostura bitters, lemon juice and soda, are popular aperitifs. Rakï (Greek *ouzo*) is widely available in the Turkish north, but not so common in the south. Every village *kafenion* has its own *zivania*, a very strong spirit that should be treated with a great deal of caution. Every autumn farmers produce their own *eau-de-vie* using private stills.

To order a Turkish coffee in a Greek café (Greek *kafenion*, Turkish *cayevi*) would be taken as a serious insult. Since the ethnic feuds, it is safe to request only Greek coffee *(kafe elliniko)*, a strong brew served in tiny cups with a thick residue of grounds.

Ripe radishes

Cypriot specialities

Soupa trahana, chicken broth served with coarsely ground wheat, soured milk, tomatoes and halloumi cheese.
Barbounia, (Turkish *barbunya*), red mullet, the tastiest and most expensive fish.
Afelia, braised or baked pork, marinated in red wine and seasoned with coriander.
Hiromeri, smoked pork.
Kleftiko (Turkish *fïrïn kebap*), lamb braised for several hours in an earthenware pot.
Lountza, loin of pork marinated in wine, grilled or fried.
Stifado, beef goulash with onions, seasoned with cinnamon.
Sheftalia, beef and pork sausages, seasoned with cinnamon and peppermint.
Dolmades or **gemista** (Turkish *dolmalar*), vegetables stuffed with rice or sometimes minced meat.
Horiatiki (Turkish *çoban salatasï*), salad with cucumber, tomatoes, onions, olives and ewes' milk cheese.
Koupepia (Turkish *yaprak dolmasï*), stuffed vine leaves.
Hummus, a thick paste made from chick peas, garlic, olive oil and lemon juice.
Tahini (Turkish *tahin*), sesame-seed paste with a dry texture like peanut butter.
Taramosalata, a mixture of cod's roe, bread soaked in milk, mashed potato and olive oil.
Halloumi (Turkish *hellim*), a salty ewes' milk cheese baked, grilled or fried.
Baklava, a sticky dessert made from filo pastry filled with almonds and cinnamon, soaked in syrup.
Soujoukko (Turkish *sucuk*), strings of almonds dipped in grape juice and left to set.

Restaurant selection

The following are suggestions for some of the most popular destinations in Cyprus. They are listed according the following price categories:
€€€ = expensive
€€ = moderate
€ = cheap

Southern Cyprus
Agia Napa
€€ Taverna Napa, Odos Dimokratias, tel: 23 721280. Traditional *taverna*, the oldest in town, uphill from the main square, with a delightful vine arbour.

Kakopetria
€€–€€€ The Mill, Odos Mylou, tel: 22 922536. Rustic style and country fare, including fresh trout, in a dizzyingly tall building next to the old mill.

Larnaka
€€ Psarolimano, 118 Odos Piyale Paşa, tel: 24 655408. By the fishing harbour. Fish *taverna* serving whatever the fishing boats catch that day. Guests can choose their fish straight from the kitchen.
€–€€ Art Café 1900, 6 Odos Stasinou, tel: 24 653027. Stylish café, bar and restaurant in a turn-of-the-20th-century house. Closed Tuesday.

Limassol
€€€ Blue Island, 3 Leoforos Amathoundos, tel: 25 321466. One of Limassol's classiest restaurants serves French and international cuisine. Formal interior and vine-shaded patio.
€€ Ladas, 31 Odos Agios Theklis, by the old harbour, tel: 25 365760. Open daily from noon. A renovated fish *taverna* that has a rustic atmosphere.
€€ Porta, 17 Odos Genethliou Mitela, tel: 25 360339. Dinner in a renovated donkey stable! Designer class and good taste prevail at this restaurant in the old Turkish quarter.

Nicosia (Lefkosia – Greek Cypriot sector)
€€ Athineon, Laïki Geitonia, tel: 22 664786. European, country-style atmosphere with stone floor, dark-stained wood and open hearth.
€ Prophyläa, 15 Odos Trikoupis, tel: 22 762669. A basic *taverna*, very lively while the produce market is open. Closed evenings and Sunday.

Pafos
€€ Pelican, 102 Leoforos Apostolou Pavlou, Kato Pafos, tel: 26 946886. Moderately good *taverna* with a superb position beside the harbour.

Popular haunt in Limassol

Family dinner
A light snack

Lunchtime in Larnaka

A wide choice of drinks

€€ Avgerinos, 4 Odos Minoön, tel: 26 932990. Near the Frankish Baths. Choose your fish, determined by the day's catch, in the kitchen. Prices are calculated by weight.

Pissouri

€€ Simposio, Pissouri Beach, tel: 25 221158. Like all restaurants here, Simposio is more expensive than it should be, but the *mezedhes* and the setting make it seem worth it.

Platres

€€ Psilodendro, uphill from the village, tel: 25 421350. Fresh farmed trout served under the shade of plane trees.
€ Kalidonia, above the village square, tel: 25 421404. Family-run concern with a big selection of traditional dishes.

Polis

€€ Karouzis, 23 Odos Verginas, tel: 26 321888, on the way to the campsite. Serves what is among the best traditional cooking in Polis.

Northern Cyprus

Alagadi Beach

€ St Kathleen's, tel: 0542 851 7640. On eastern edge of Alagadi village. A simple restaurant with vine arbour.

Bogazi (Boğaz)

€ Kemal'ın Yeri, seafront, tel: 371 2515. Bedecked in maritime trophies and photos of football teams and film stars.

Famagusta (Ammochostos/Gazimağusa)

€€ Cyprus House, Polat Paşa Bulvarı, tel: 366 4845. Traditional Turkish Cypriot fare served in the former colonial-era police station. Open for lunch and dinner. Closed Sunday.
€€ Petek Pastanesi, Yeşildeniz Sokaği, tel: 366 4304. Café that's open from early in the morning until late at night. Appetising delicacies beautifully arranged in long window displays. Meeting place for the young and well-heeled.

Karmi

€€€ Treasure, tel: 822 2400. In the former village school, furnished with valuable antiques. Closed Wednesday.

Keryneia (Girne)

€€€ Harbour Club, Old Harbour, tel: 815 2211. Meeting place for sailors with some fine views of the harbour.
€€ Grapevine, tel: 815 2496. Ecevit Cad. 25. International cuisine. Sit under an attractive vine canopy. Closed Sunday.

Morfou (Güzelyurt)

€ Şah, near the entrance to the town from Keryneia, tel: 714 3064. *Mezedhes* and kebabs, music at the weekend.

Nicosia (Lefkoşa – Turkish Cypriot sector)
€€ El Sabor Latino, Selimiye Meydanı, tel: 228 8322. Excellent Mediterranean cuisine served in continental café-style surroundings, one of the 'in' places. Live piano music on Saturday nights. Open Mon–Sat 10am–midnight.
€€ Konak, Selimiye Meydanı, tel: 229 1212. International dishes in a lovingly restored historic mansion in the shadow of the main city centre mosque.

Nightlife

Southern Cyprus

For many visitors, Cypriot nightlife means a visit to a 'traditional Cypriot show' that invariably ends up with the audience dancing a tipsy and none-too-skilful *Zorba the Greek*, or the *karaoke* bars of the resorts. Agia Napa has sprung from nowhere to become one of Europe's hottest summer clubbing venues, in line with the likes of Ibiza and Faliraki on Rhodes – but for how long? Clubs frequently change their name and their look so as to avoid becoming last year's 'hot' place. Many locals don't like the clubs much, neither do visiting families with children, but there are lots of high-spirited young people in search of a fun holiday who would disagree. An associated problem of drugs and rowdiness has developed, something once almost unheard of in Cyprus: the police have adopted a zero-tolerance approach to both.

Though lacking in international cachet, Limassol and Pafos have their own raucous entertainment districts: Limassol's at the Potamos Germasogeias hotel district, and Pafos's around the bar strip in Kato Pafos. Nicosia – and to a lesser degree Larnaka – has a more sophisticated scene, with a scattering of clubs that appeal more to Cypriots.

Afternoon cocktails

Late-night distractions

Northern Cyprus
An evening out at the local belly-dancing club is the Turkish Cypriot sector's answer to *Zorba*. Keryneia (Girne) has the most active nightclubs scene in the North, followed by Famagusta outside of the Old Town and northern Nicosia.

Beaches in the North are quieter

Active Holidays

Beaches
As an island, Cyprus can offer plenty of beaches. The sandy beaches in the south, chiefly around Agia Napa and also in the Larnaka and Limassol region, can be very busy during the summer, as can the beaches in the west around Pafos. The North is less developed and usually much quieter.

Watersports
Wrecks, amphorae and other sunken relics left by ancient seafarers are just waiting to be discovered and **divers** will receive useful tips from the diving schools and clubs in Keryneia, Pafos, Pissouri, Paralimni, Agia Napa and Lakki. It may be possible to hire equipment too. All discoveries must be declared and it is illegal to take sponges. Since the opening of the Suez Canal, many colourful fish native to the Indian and Pacific Oceans have joined the 50 or so species native to Cypriot waters.

During the summer, Cyprus is an ideal place to learn to **windsurf** or **sail**. Along the south coast a reliable, onshore wind starts blowing late in the morning and continues until about 5pm. Boards and dinghies can usually be hired from the beach hotels. The sea around Cyprus is too calm for more advanced windsurfing. Well-equipped marinas can be found in Limassol, Larnaka and Keryneia.

Life in the slow lane

Horse-riding
Riding has become an increasingly popular pastime with riding schools and stables opening at or near major resorts. Exploring along the coast but away from the main beaches, in the cool of late afternoon, makes for a pleasant excursion. You can discover the countryside around Keryneia, Bogazi, Famagusta, Nicosia, Limassol and Pafos on horseback.

Skiing
With the sea only a short drive from the mountains, an unusual opportunity exists during the winter to take a dip in the (somewhat chilly) Mediterranean in the morning and to go **skiing** in the afternoon. The slopes of Mount Olympos (1,951m/6,401ft), known to the locals as 'frost-bite' *(chionistra)*, are equipped with ski-lifts. The skiing season can last until mid-March and Cyprus Ski Club centres will loan skiing equipment, as will some of the hotels in the Troodos.

On the road

Cycling

Anyone who is fit and active enough to handle the hills and the heat should enjoy a **cycle tour**. In the South, the Troodos and the hilly regions in the west make good cycling country, as do the Karpasia peninsula and the ridge of the Pentadaktylos mountains. These days, most bikes for hire are either mountain bikes or hybrid touring bikes, but they may be in far from ideal condition. Serious cyclists can also bring their own bikes, unless they have specifically booked a cycling tour. At least eight gears are recommended and tyres should not be too narrow.

Walking

Enjoying the countryside on foot is an alien concept to most Cypriots, although the mountains or the deserted Akamas and Karpasia peninsulas make good walking country.

The Pafos hinterland has been identified by some travel companies as good walking country and the tourist office there has a list of the available tours. A forest track was laid by the British along the Pentadaktylos ridge; walkers here will appreciate both the shade of the trees and the views.

The terrain in Cyprus is not especially difficult, although the ground is often stony and covered with thick undergrowth. Stout walking shoes are recommended, together with trousers to protect against thorny bushes. A 1:25000 map will help but no footpaths are shown. The old bridle paths are still used in the Turkish North, but in the South most of them have reverted to their natural state. However, on the Akamas peninsula and in the Troodos, for example, the authorities have laid out and waymarked a number of nature trails. Leaflets are usually provided in boxes at the start of the walks with guidance on the flora and geological features encountered en route. Spring and autumn are the best times for walking holidays, although the summer heat is bearable high up in the Troodos and Pentadaktylos mountains.

Enjoying the Cyprus scenery

Getting to the Greek Cypriot sector

By air

There are direct air links to Cyprus from most European countries and from many in the Middle East. The national airline, Cyprus Airways (in the UK, tel: 020 8359 1333; in Cyprus, tel: 22 365700), operates direct flights to Larnaka from London (Heathrow, Gatwick and Stansted), Birmingham and Manchester. There is another airport at Pafos, which also serves these British cities.

Since the liberalisation of air travel to Cyprus, the number of operators offering flights between central Europe and the Mediterranean islands has increased. Many Middle Eastern companies, for example, have obtained carrier licences.

By boat

The car-ferry service from Greece (Rhodes, Piraeus, Crete) and Israel (Haifa) to Lemesos (Limassol) has been 'temporarily' suspended since 2003. There are no indications as to when, if ever, it will restart. Private cars can currently be shipped only on cargo vessels.

Opposite: Cyprus hues

Lanarka airport

Getting to the Turkish Cypriot sector

By air

North Cyprus's airline is Cyprus Turkish Airlines (in the UK 020 7930 4851; in Cyprus 227 1706). Because of the international boycott, Turkish Airlines and Istanbul Airlines are the only other airlines that operate to northern Cyprus. Most flights make a stop in Istanbul or Izmir. The main airport for northern Cyprus is at Ercan, 25km (16 miles) from Nicosia (Lefkoşa), but some flights arrive at Geçitkale, 30km (19 miles) northwest of Famagusta (Ammochostos/ Gazimağusa).

By boat

Ferries to northern Cyprus leave only from Turkey. Ferries leave Alanya and Silifke-Taşucu for Keryneia (Girne); the national ferry company TML links Mersin with Famagusta. Between May and October a hovercraft runs three times a week from Taşucu. The journey takes about 8 hours, usually overnight, with a 20 percent reduction offered to students.

Despite the liberalisation of movement across the buffer zone in recent years, those who go directly to northern Cyprus still cannot visit the southern part of the island on the same trip. The Republic of Cyprus continues to regard direct entry into North Cyprus as an illegal act. The exception to the rule are nationals of other EU member countries, allowed to do so since the Greek Cypriot-administered republic entered the European Union in May 2004.

Getting Around

By bus and taxi

An old campaigner

Buses on scheduled services run between the main towns, Monday–Saturday. The companies and their routes are: **Lefkosia Interurban Buses**, tel: 22 665814; Lefkosia–Lemesos and return. **K. Interurban Buses**, tel: 24 643492, 24 722700, 24 665814; Lefkosia–Larnaka and return, Lemesos–Larnaka and return. **Nea Amoroza Transport**, tel: 26 936822, 26 936740; Pafos–Polis and return. **E.P.A.**, tel: 23 821318, 23 825607, 99 484818; Paralimni–Protaras–Larnaka and return. **Eman Buses**, tel: 23 721321; Agia Napa–Larnaka and return.

There are regular bus services run by private operators (e.g. Costas, ALEPA and KEMEK) between the main towns. Good bus services also connect the main towns with Polis, Platres, Troodos village, Agia Napa and Kakopetria. The buses leave from either the towns' main bus stations or outside the offices of the individual operator concerned.

Visitors might still see a few old buses, many of them dating from the post-war era and, lovingly painted in red and green, looking like museum pieces. These buses serve most villages but are timed to meet the needs of the locals, e.g. an early-morning run into town and then back at lunch-time.

Service taxis are minibuses that operate scheduled services between the main towns. The passenger books the taxi by phone, is picked up and taken to his or her destination. Service taxis are operated by **Pagkypria Eteria Yperastikon Taxi** (Cyprus Interurban Taxi Company). For reservations contact the company at the following locations: Municipal Parking, Leoforos Salaminos, Kolokasi, Nicosia (Lefkosia), tel: 22 730888; corner of Odos Papakyriakou and Odos Marsellou, Larnaka, tel: 24 661010 and corner of Odos Kitiou and Odos Kilkis, tel: 24 662110; 21a Odos Thessalonikis, Limassol (Lemessos), tel: 77777474 and corner of Odos Kavazoglou and Odos Misiaouli, tel: 25 877666; 34 Odos Kinyras, Pafos, tel: 26 923800.

Routes available are: Lefkosia–Lemesos; Lemesos–LefkosiaLarnaka–Lefkosia; Lefkosia–Larnaka and Larnaka airport; Larnaka–Lemesos; Lemesos–Larnaka and Larnaka airport; Lemesos–Pafos; Pafos–Lemesos; Lemesos-Pafos airport.

The **dolmuş**, the Turkish version of the service taxi, is popular in the north and arrived in northern Cyprus via the latest wave of Anatolian immigrants. *Dolmuşular*, or 'full up' – they only leave when all seats are full – are mainly used on the Nicosia–Keryneia (Girne) and Nicosia–Famagusta (Gazimağusa) routes. For visitors travelling from the South to the North the regular minibus service that connects Nicosia with Keryneia and, less frequently, with Famagusta, is a good way to go.

Trips to the North

With the opening of the intra-island border at the Ledra Palace Hotel in Nicosia in 2003, travel from South to North has become much easier. New crossing points have been opened along the length of the demarcation line – in 2005 a total of six were either open or being prepared. Visitors can travel quite easily under their own steam, but many will prefer to go on an organised tour. These three-day long excursions are recommended for visitors staying in the South of the island but wanting to visit the North (*see Routes 12–16*):

- •Keryneia and then to Hilarion fortress and Belapaïs Abbey *(see page 59)*
- •Famagusta, Salamis and the Varnavas monastery *(see page 68)*
- •Soloi and Vouni Palace (*see pages 64–5*)

Rental cars and minibuses hired in the South are able to cross the border into the North. Taxis are the easiest way of getting around northern Cyprus; cabs also wait at the border crossings or on Atatürk Meydanı in North Nicosia.

Vehicle hire

The main car-hire firms have offices in all the tourist centres. The price, costlier in the South and in the high season, includes unlimited mileage and comprehensive insurance. Punctures, broken windscreens and sump damage are not included in the insurance. Those intending to go off road should therefore consider a four-wheel-drive vehicle. Drivers must be 21 years of age; anyone above the age of 70 will have difficulty obtaining a hire car. An international driving licence is not required. Many tour operators will book a hire car in advance if requested.

Driving is on the left. The legal alcohol limit for drivers in the South is 90mg alcohol per 100ml of blood and 39mg alcohol per 100ml of breath; in the North the limit is 50mg alcohol per 100ml of breath. Top speed on the motorway is 100kmph (62mph), on other trunk roads 80kmph (50mph) – 40–60kmph (25–37mph) in the North – and in built-up areas 50kmph (31mph). Radar speed checks are in use on some motoways and also on the Nicosia by-pass.

A choice of routes

Many petrol stations in the South are equipped with machines which accept C£5 or C£10 notes, so you can fill up with fuel on a Sunday. Take care to set off with a full tank if touring the Karpasia peninsula in the North which at present has only three petrol stations. Be prepared for the unexpected, such as a broken petrol pump. Be friendly to local farmers – you may need their help in the event of a mishap! Drivers taking their **own car** to Cyprus must have Cypriot third-party liability insurance. Many foreign insurance policies, along with a Green Card, are acceptable. Cars licensed abroad may be used on Cypriot roads for three months tax-free; apply to the main customs office for an extension.

Travel documents

To enter Cyprus a passport valid for at least three more months is required. A special visa is not needed.

Citizens of the European Union can travel without restriction throughout Cyprus, so long as local rules and exceptions are respected, and they have arrived at an airport or port recognised by the Republic of Cyprus as a legal port of entry. EU nationals are now allowed to cross from the North into the South. Visitors to the South are now allowed to cross freely into the North. Some restrictions may be retained for non-EU citizens wishing to travel in either direction, but as travel between the two sections is increasingly being liberalised (as of summer 2005), both the rules and the policy on their enforcement is subject to change. Crossings may be made on foot in Nicosia at the Ledra Palace Hotel checkpoint and by vehicle at Agios Dometios/Metehan, near Nicosia; and at Famagusta. At the time of writing, new crossing points are due to open soon in Nicosia city centre and near Morfou (Güzelyurt).

Customs

For residents of the European Union, there are no restrictions on the import of (legal) goods for personal use. Generous guideline amounts exist for what constitutes personal use. The following goods may be imported duty-free into southern Cyprus: 50 cigars, 200 cigarettes or 250g tobacco; 1 litre spirits; 2 litres wine; 50cl perfume, and 250cl eau de toilette; and other items apart from jewellery up to the value of C£175. Entering northern Cyprus, the limits are 400 cigarettes or equivalent; 1 litre spirits; 1 litre wine; 100cl perfume; and personal goods up to the value of €135 or equivalent.

The export of antiquities is forbidden and offenders are severely punished.

Tourist information

For tourist information about southern Cyprus, contact the nearest office of the Cyprus Tourism Organisation:
UK: Cyprus Tourist Office, 17 Hanover Street, London W1S 1YP, tel: 020 7569 8800; fax: 020 7499 4935; e-mail: informationcto@btconnect.com; www.visitcyprus.org.cy.
US: Cyprus Tourism Organisation, 13 E 40th Street, New York, NY10016, tel: 212 683 5280; fax: 212 683 5282; e-mail: gocyprus@aol.com; www.visitcyprus.org.cy.

Northern Cyprus tourist offices are:
UK: 29 Bedford Square, London WC1B 3EG, tel: 020 7631 1930; fax: 020 7462 9789; e-mail: info@go-northcyprus.com; www.tourism.trnc.net.
US: 1667 K Street, Suite 690, Washington DC 20006, tel:

202 887 6198; fax: 202 467 0685; e-mail: kktc@orels.com; www.tourism.trnc.net.

Ministry of Communications, Public Works and Tourism, Idris Doğan Sokaği, Lefkoşa (postal address: Mersin 10, Turkey), tel: 228 9629; fax: 227 3976.

Southern Cyprus
The CTO offices in Nicosia, Limassol, Larnaka, Pafos, Agia Napa, Polis and Platres will be happy to help.
Head office: PO Box 24535, 19 Leoforos Lemesou, 1390 Nicosia, tel: 22 691100; fax: 22 331644; e-mail: cytour@cto.org.cy; www.visitcyprus.org.cy (written requests for information only).
Agia Napa: 12 Leoforos Kryou Nerou, tel: 23 721796. **Larnaka**: Plateia Vasileos Pavlou, tel: 24 654322. The tourist office at the airport is manned for all incoming flights. **Limassol**: 115a Odos Spyrou Araouzou, tel: 25 362756. Near the castle. 22 Odos Georgiou A', Potamos tis Germasogeias, tel: 25 323211. The tourist office at the harbour is manned for all arriving cruise ships. **Nicosia**: 35 Aristokyprou, Laïki Geitonia, near Plateia Eleftherias, tel: 02 444264. **Pafos**: 3 Odos Gladstonos, Ktima, 63a Leoforos Poseidonos, Kato Pafos, tel: 26 930521. The tourist office at the airport is manned for all incoming flights. **Polis**: 2 Odos Vasileos Stasioikou, tel: 26 322468. **Platres**: in the village centre, tel: 25 421316.

Northern Cyprus
Nicosia (Lefkoşa): an office at the Girne Gate operates sporadically; the permanent office is at the Tourist Ministry, tel: 22 89629; e-mail: info@holidayinnorthcyprus.com; www.holidayinnorthcyprus.com. **Famagusta (Gazimağusa)**: Fevzi Çakmak Bulvarı, tel: 366 2864. **Keryneia (Girne)** Kordon Boyu, tel: 815 2145. By the harbour.

Currency and exchange

The unit of currency in southern Cyprus is the Cypriot pound (C£). It is divided into 100 cents. Banks and hotels accept traveller's cheques and the main credit cards. Visa, MasterCard, American Express, Diners Club and EC card holders may withdraw cash from cash dispensers. In 2005, Cyprus took the first official step towards replacing the Cyprus pound with the euro, predicted for 2008.

The currency used in the North is the new Turkish lira (YTL). Hotels will change traveller's cheques but will charge a commission of up to 5 percent. State-licensed *bureaux de change* usually stay open at weekends. MasterCard, Visa, American Express and Diners Club cards are accepted.

No more than C£50 may be taken out of southern Cyprus, but there is no limit on the import of C£ and foreign currencies, though cash of the value of €12,500 or more

Lace is popular

should be declared on entry. In the North, there is no limit to the amount of lira which may be imported, but exports are restricted to no more than $3,000 or its equivalent.

Opening times

Southern Cyprus

Banks: Monday to Friday 8.30am–12.30pm, in Nicosia and the tourist centres also Monday to Friday 4–6.30pm (October to April, 3.30–5.30pm).

Government offices, post offices: Monday to Friday 7.30am–1.30pm, Thursday also 3–6pm.

Shops: Monday to Saturday 8am–1pm and 4–7pm (October to April, 2.30–5.30pm). Closed Wednesday and Saturday afternoon. In the tourist centres souvenir shops and other tourist-orientated outlets stay open until late.

Northern Cyprus

Banks: Monday to Friday 8.30am–noon and 2.30–4pm.

Government offices: October to April Monday to Friday 8am–1pm and 2.30–5pm; May to September Monday to Friday 7.30am–2pm, also Monday 3.30–6pm.

Shops: in summer, Monday to Saturday 8am–1pm and 4–7pm; in winter, Monday to Saturday 8am–1pm and 2–6pm; food shops stay open every day until about 8pm.

Post offices: Monday to Friday 8am–1pm and 2–5pm.

Public holidays

Southern Cyprus

New Year's Day; Epiphany; 25 March (Greek Independence Day); 1 April (Greek Cypriot National Day); 1 May; 15 August (Assumption Day); 1 October (Cyprus Independence Day); 28 October (Greek National Day); 25/26 December.

Green (or Shrove) Monday, Good Friday, Easter Saturday, Easter Sunday, Easter Monday and Whitsuntide are calculated according to the Orthodox Julian calendar and consequently do not correspond with the same festivals of the Western church. Dates vary each year.

Northern Cyprus

New Year's Day; 23 April (Turkish Independence and Children's Day); 1 May; 19 May (Youth and Sports Festival); 20 July (Peace and Freedom Day, to commemorate the invasion of 1974); 1 August (War of Liberation Day); 30 August (Turkish Victory over Greece in 1922); 29 October (Turkish National Day); 15 November (Turkish Cypriot National Day).

The main Muslim religious festivals observed in Turkish Cyprus follow the cycles of the moon and occur 10 to 15 days earlier each year. Both the two main festivals – Şeker Bayramı (at the end of Ramadan) and Kurban Bayramı (Birthday of the Prophet) – last for three to five days.

Shopping and souvenirs

Shopping in Cyprus follows the European practice, so haggling over marked prices is not normally acceptable.

Traditional souvenirs from **southern Cyprus** are the colourful woven goods and Lefkara lace. Clay pottery and engraved copper vessels or brass plates are also reasonably priced. *Soujoukko*, strings of nuts dipped in grape juice, are popular with youngsters, as are *glyko*, fruit soaked in syrup, while *Commandaria*, a sweet wine, is often appreciated by older people. The Cyprus Handicraft Service shops run by the Ministry of Trade and Industry are good places to see the full range of locally produced crafts.

Portable souvenirs

Popular souvenirs available in **northern Cyprus** include embroidery, carpets *(kelim)* and wickerwork (made from grasses or reeds). Leather goods are often good value (but always check the quality of the sewing) and gold jewellery is also relatively cheap.

Postal services

In northern Cyprus enquire about prices at a post office or in a hotel as the cost of postage has increased several times in a year because of currency devaluations. Northern Cyprus is not a member of the Universal Postal Union and so all mail to foreign destinations has to pass through Turkey. Do not write Cyprus on any mail to northern Cyprus as it will arrive in southern Cyprus and not be forwarded. Instead of 'Cyprus', write 'Mersin 10, Turkey'.

Telephone

To call a number in southern Cyprus, dial the country code 357 and then the full number. There are no area codes in the South. For non-EU citizens, the telephone connections to northern Cyprus are made via Turkey: dial the Turkish dialling code 90, followed by 392 (the dialling code covering the whole of northern Cyprus), then the number of the party you wish to reach. For mobile phones, dial the Turkish dialling code 90, followed by 542 or 533 (depending on mobile phone service provider), then the number.

Southern Cyprus

Coin-operated public telephones (5, 10, 20 cent coins) have mostly been replaced by call boxes which only accept phone cards, sold in telephone offices, post offices and banks.

Northern Cyprus

It is possible to make international calls from all phone boxes. Payphones in the North now only accept phone cards, sold in denominations of 100, 200 and 300 units. These are currently priced, respectively, at 4.85YTL, 8.15YTL and 11.45YTL. No dialling prefix is necessary when phoning within northern Cyprus.

Time
Cyprus is two hours ahead of GMT. In summer the clocks run one hour ahead.

Electricity
Electricity is supplied at 220–240V AC. Generally, electrical outlets correspond to British standards.

Units of measure
Cyprus, North and South, uses the metric system of weights and measures, but also uses traditional units, such as the *oka* (1.24kg), used at the market, and *dönüm* (1.1ha).

Nudism and topless sunbathing
Pretty well anything goes on the beaches in the Greek Cypriot sector as long as a small patch of material covers the private parts. In Cyprus nobody goes into the water totally naked, at least not where others can watch.

In the Turkish Cypriot sector, the rules are stricter and topless bathing is only acceptable on hotel beaches.

Frenaros Church, Agia Napa

Churches and monasteries
When visiting churches, monasteries or mosques, men and women should cover their shoulders and knees. In some monasteries that receive a large number of visitors, staff will issue shawls or cloaks if necessary. It is considered offensive for visitors to turn their back on an iconostasis. The room behind it is reserved for the priest and only men are permitted to enter. If a church has been opened specially, a small donation or the purchase of a candle is expected. Kissing icons would be regarded as excessive.

Photography
Taking photographs and using video cameras in state-owned museums is allowed only with a special permit, but you may generally take photographs at archaeological sites, with the exception of one or two new digs where details of all the finds have not yet been published. Photographing or filming the area around the Green Line, other military installations and soldiers is strictly forbidden.

Language
English is widely understood in Cyprus.

Tipping
A 10 percent tip on top of a restaurant bill is normal, while taxi drivers look forward to receiving a rounded-up amount for the fare. Room staff in hotels also expect a small tip.

Newspapers
Foreign newspapers usually arrive in Cyprus with a delay of

one or two days. The daily *Cyprus Mail* and the *Cyprus Weekly* are English-language papers. In the North, there's the weekly English-language *Cyprus Today*.

Selling yesterday's news

Medical assistance

Many Cypriot doctors are trained in Britain and therefore speak English. Normal consulting times are Monday to Friday 9am–1pm and 4–7pm. Details of the night-time emergency service and which doctors are on call at the weekend are given in the daily newspapers and in southern Cyprus by phoning 192.

Good private insurance is advisable. Medical consultations, hospital fees and medicines have to be paid for at once.

Disabled

The Pancyprian Organisation for Disabled Persons, 50 Odos Pendelis Strovolos, PO Box 2013, Nicosia, tel: 22 426301, can assist disabled travellers.

Emergencies

Dial 112 in **southern Cyprus** for police, fire brigade and first aid. In **northern Cyprus**, dial 155 for police, 199 in case of fire, 112 for an ambulance.

Forest fires

During the dry season, Cyprus is plagued by forest fires. Discarded cigarette ends or the careless use of barbecues often turn out to be the cause. Take care, especially when signs indicate high fire risk. In the Troodos mountain range there is an emergency forest telephone network for notifying the forest rangers of any fires. In northern Cyprus, call the special hotline 177 to report a forest fire.

Heed the fire warnings

Diplomatic representation

UK: High Commission, Odos Alexandrou Palli, Nicosia, tel: 22 861100.
USA: Embassy, corner of Odos Metochiou and Odos Ploutarchou, Egkomi, Nicosia, tel: 22 776400.
Australia: High Commission, 4 Odos Annis Komninis, Nicosia, tel: 22 753001.
Ireland: Chancery, 7 Odos Aiantas, Nicosia, tel: 22 818183.

Because **northern Cyprus** is not recognised as an independent country (other than by Turkey), no reciprocal exchange exists between ambassadors or consuls. But representatives can be found at the following offices:
UK: British High Commission, 23 Mehmet Akif Avenue, tel: 28 83862.
US: American Centre, 6 Saran Street, tel: 22 73930.
Australia: Australian Representation Division, 20 Güner Türkmen Street, tel: 22 77332.

Accommodation

The boom in hotel construction continues apace in the South and new, good-quality hotels open every year. In the North the range of accommodation is more limited, but increasing all the time.

In the Greek Cypriot sector

Modern development, Agia Napa

For a long time Agia Napa/Paralimni and Limassol saw the bulk of new holiday development, but in recent years Pafos has emerged as the tourists' favourite resort. Fewer hotel beds are found in Nicosia, Polis and the Troodos. All hotels, holiday apartments and campsites are regulated by the tourist board (*see pages 94–5*), who will send a list of accommodation available.

Hotels are categorised according to a one- to five-star system. There's something of a glut of hotels in the higher stars categories, and relatively fewer good places further down the chain. Overnight tariffs as laid down by the authorities are displayed in all rooms. In the low season from November to Easter (May in the mountains), most hotels will negotiate a reduction.

Self-catering accommodation ranges from smart villas by the sea to simple flats in urban apartment blocks. The advantage of this kind of accommodation, of course, is having access to a cooker, which obviates the need to go out for every meal. Visitors are advised to book such accommodation through a reputable travel company. Because of government regulations, accommodation in private rooms is hard to come by.

Youth hostels exist in Nicosia, Larnaka, Pafos and Troodos. For further details or group bookings contact: Cyprus Youth Hostel Association, PO Box 24040, 1700 Nicosia, tel: 22 670027, fax: 22 672896 .

Campsites by the coast have plenty of space even in high season. Camping is popular with Cypriots, but in summer they opt for the mountains rather than the seaside. The Troodos campsite, situated in pine woods, is a good place to make contact with the locals. The forestry authorities in the mountains permit walkers to camp at official picnic sites, where basic facilities are provided.

In the Turkish Cypriot sector

Hotels and **villas** in this sector are also classified according to a star system, but the hoteliers themselves award the stars and are often rather generous when assessing their own establishment. Travelling independently in northern Cyprus is probably cheaper than arranging rooms through a travel agent.

The hotel complexes on the east coast (in and around Famagusta) overlook miles of sandy beaches, but the flat hinterland is not so attractive. Keryneia is a different matter. As the mountains are within easy reach, there are plenty of opportunities for walks, but the beaches do not compare with those on the east coast. On the Karpasia peninsula you will find beds in rather basic hostels.

Self-catering accommodation is restricted to the north coast around Keryneia. Of the rather limited choice, the holiday villas and apartments in Karmi, an idyllic village on the slopes of the Beşparmak mountains, are by far the best. Private rooms are not normally available.

Proper **campsites** are located near Famagusta and Keryneia. *Camping sauvage* is permitted and Cypriots in the North derive the same pleasure as their southern counterparts from pitching their tents at picnic sites in the Beşparmak mountains. Visitors should be aware that there may be restrictions near other military installations and prohibited zones.

Hotel selection

The following are hotel suggestions for some of the most popular spots, listed according to three categories: **€€€** = expensive; **€€** = moderate; **€** = cheap

A tasteful complex in the North

Southern Cyprus

Agia Napa

€€€ Nissi Beach, 3km (2 miles) from the centre by Nissi Bay, tel: 23 721021, fax: 23 721623, www.nissi-beach.com. Large garden, own watersports centre, freshwater swimming pool, tennis courts. Disco and nightclub are situated well away from the bedrooms. **€€ Cornelia**, 23 Leoforos Makariou, tel: 23 721406, fax: 23 722409. Central location.

High season in Agia Napa

Agros

€€ Rodon Hotel, Odos Rodou, tel: 25 521201, fax: 25 521235, www.rodonhotel.com. A modern hotel on the edge of the village, with swimming pool and garden. Half-board only in high season.

Drouseia

€€ Cyprotel Droushia Heights, tel: 26 332351, fax: 26 332353, www.dhcyprotels.com. On the edge of the village. Fine views and rustic furnishings. Self-catering apartments.

Kakopetria

€€ Linos Inn, 34 Odos Palaias, tel 22 923161, fax: 22 923181, www.linos-inn.com.cy. Hotel in a renovated traditional house in the centre of the village.

Lakki

€ Aphrodite Beach, tel: 26 321001, fax: 26 322015. Close to the beach, 2km (1 mile) from the Baths of Aphrodite.

Old Famagusta

The Dome Hotel

Larnaka

€€€ Golden Bay, Dekeleia Road, 10km (7 miles) along the coast to the east, tel: 24 645444, fax: 24 645451, www.lordos.com.cy. The best hotel in the town. **€ Sandbeach Castle**, Odos Piyale Paşa, tel: 24 655437, fax: 24 659804, www.castlehotel.com.cy. Unusual architectural design.

Limassol

€€ Curium Palace, 2 Odos Vyronos, tel: 25 891100, fax: 25 635300, www.curiumpalace.com. Urban hotel but with garden and swimming pool. **€ Continental**, 115 Odos Spyrou Araouzou, tel: 25 362530, 25 362534, fax: 25 373030. Basic, older-style hotel with a popular café on the promenade.

Nicosia (Lefkosia – Greek Cypriot sector)

€€€ Holiday Inn, 70 Odos Rigainis, tel: 22 712712, fax: 22 673337, www.holiday-inn-cyprus.com. Best hotel in the old town. Fine view from the roof terrace (with swimming pool). **€ Averof**, tel: 22 773447, fax: 22 773411, www.averof.com.cy. In a residential area to the west, 15 minutes' walk from the town centre. Furnished in country style.

Pafos

€€€ Cypria Maris, tel: 26 964111, fax: 26 964125, www.riuhotels.com. A lively, luxury hotel with sandy beach. **€€ Roman**, Odos Agios Lambrianou, tel: 26 945411, fax: 26 946834, www.romanhotel.com.cy. Between Ktima and Kato Pafos at the start of the road to Coral Bay. Internal furnishings in ancient Roman style. **€ Axiothea**, 2 Odos Ivi Malioti, tel: 26 932866, fax: 26 945790. Family-run concern, rooms with fine views.

Pissouri

€ Bunch of Grapes Inn, 9 Odos Ioannou Erotokritou, tel: 25 221275, fax: 25 22 2510. Just 11 rooms in the village, huddled round a courtyard shaded by vines.

Platres

€€€ Forest Park, 1km (⅔ mile) outside the town towards Prodromos, tel: 25 421751, fax: 25 421875, www.forestparkhotel.com.cy. Colonial-style hotel with swimming pool. **€ Minerva**, 10-minute walk from the town centre, tel: 25 421731, fax: 25 421075. Ideal for walkers and nature-lovers.

Polis

€ Bougainvillea, 13 Odos Verginas, tel: 26 812250, fax: 26 322203, www.bougainvillea.com.cy. A peaceful apartment hotel with garden and swimming pool.

Protaras

€€ Louis Ayios Elias Holiday Village, 44 Odos Profitis